The Nuts & Bolts of College Writing

Third Edition

The Nuts & Bolts of College Writing

Third Edition

Michael Harvey

Hackett Publishing Company, Inc.
Indianapolis/Cambridge

For further information, please address
    Hackett Publishing Company, Inc.
    P.O. Box 44937
    Indianapolis, Indiana 46244-0937

    www.hackettpublishing.com

Composition by Integrated Composition Systems
Cover design by E. L. Wilson

Library of Congress Control Number: 2020934811

ISBN-13: 978-1-62466-919-4 (cloth)
ISBN-13: 978-1-62466-859-3 (pbk.)

For George Orwell,
who matters more than ever

There was a sociologist who had written a paper for us all to read—something he had written ahead of time. I started to read the damn thing, and my eyes were coming out: I couldn't make head nor tail of it! I figured it was because I hadn't read any of the books on [the conference] list. I had this uneasy feeling of "I'm not adequate," until finally I said to myself, "I'm gonna stop, and read *one sentence* slowly, so I can figure out what the hell it means."

So I stopped—at random—and read the next sentence very carefully. I can't remember it precisely, but it was very close to this: "The individual member of the social community often receives his information via visual, symbolic channels." I went back and forth over it, and translated. You know what it means? "People read."

Then I went over the next sentence, and I realized that I could translate that one also. Then it became a kind of empty business: "Sometimes people read; sometimes people listen to the radio," and so on, but written in such a fancy way that I couldn't understand it at first, and when I finally deciphered it, there was nothing to it.

Nobel Prize–winning physicist Richard Feynman,
"Surely You're Joking, Mr. Feynman!":
Adventures of a Curious Character (1985)

Modern English, especially written English, is full of bad habits which spread by imitation and which can be avoided if one is willing to take the necessary trouble. If one gets rid of these habits one can think more clearly.

George Orwell, "Politics and the
English Language" (1946)

You don't start out writing good stuff. You start out writing crap and thinking it's good stuff, and then gradually you get better at it.

Octavia E. Butler, interview,
Locus Magazine (2000)

A word after a word
after a word is power.

Margaret Atwood, "Spelling" (1981)

Contents

Introduction to the Third Edition

EXPECTATIONS ABOUT WRITING college essays have changed since the first edition of this book was published seventeen years ago. Today there is much more attention to issues of correctness—that is to say, to using non-offensive and inclusive language to refer to people (and other beings).[1] Identifiers of race, nationality, ethnicity, sexuality, age, religion, ability, and more—but gender in particular—have become a tangle of rules, expectations, and opportunities for advocacy or offense for writers and readers. If one is writing about menstruation, for instance, the term "people with periods" now presents itself as an inclusive substitute for the word that once would have been automatically used for those who experience it, "women." It is easy to deride such innovations, but it is also easy to see their logicality and even aptness: As our understanding of identity expands, should not our language expand as well?

In many ways this is exciting and serves as an invitation to ponder the power of words to obscure or to reveal, to harm or to help, and to shape our very thoughts. Language, both spoken and written, has always been a battleground pitting new ideas, values, and experiments against the hard-won judgments and lessons of the past. Contesting particular words has always been a part of the battle. And claims of correctness are always ideological, whoever makes them. Now to term something "ideological" is not in and of itself a criticism—but it does suggest that part of our job as writers and readers is to be attuned to this non-neutral aspect of the words we and others choose. As the unapologetically political—but always independent-minded—English writer George Orwell, to whom this book is dedicated, said, "The more one is conscious of one's political bias, the more chance one has of acting politically without sacrificing one's aesthetic and intellectual integrity" (1956, 394).

---

1. With regard to animals, see the inaugural editorial in the *Journal of Animal Ethics*, which advises contributors to the journal to avoid the term "pets" as patronizing and ethically misleading, and suggests the term "companion animals" as its replacement ("Terms of Discourse," *Journal of Animal Ethics*, vol. 1, no. 1, Spring 2011, pp. vii–ix).

This book is meant to help you write college essays with both effectiveness and integrity. Its advice on correctness is to think fairly, to write clearly—and prudently to ask your teachers what set of conventions they expect you to follow. Once you are past us well-meaning custodians of correctness, you will have more freedom. Of course it will not come as a surprise that your freedom will then be challenged by a world with its own demands and exhortations about how you should write and what words you must or must not use—and that the particulars will change according to time, place, and fashion.

Even in that wider world, however, it is my hope that the chief lesson of this book—to be clear in your writing about who does what—will prove its lasting worth. Society evolves, technology advances, and human potential increases: but the human condition persists. We live as our species has always lived: born in tears, learning hard lessons about the difficulty of communication and the fragility of cooperation, and struggling to understand and be understood. In the course of our lives all of us, for better or worse, will face countless choices with significant moral consequences. Anyone who writes expository essays about life and striving is telling a story about actions and choices. The best (most effective *and* most moral) way to do this will always be a baseline style of active voice and strong verbs that helps clarify who has done what, to whom, with what consequence. This is not meant to restrict your creativity—please, feel free to experiment and play with words all you want—that's part of the joy of language! But it is meant to alert you to the basic moral responsibility of good expository writing: it should reveal, not obscure. At least, that's my advice. In the end, it's your choice.

Introduction

THIS BOOK CAN help you write better college essays. It combines the most important rules and conventions of academic writing with the rudiments of good style. Naturally it has its limitations: it is general (with little to say about writing in different disciplines), basic (and may be most useful to beginning college students), and short (thus covering a lot of ground quickly). It is not about critical thinking in any formal sense, and indeed tries to lay down its do's and don'ts, as well as my own unauthorized views on writing, as informally as possible. These views, personal and perhaps even idiosyncratic, may be its biggest limitation. Yet writing is an intensely personal activity. It seems only right, even necessary, that writing advice have a personal touch as well.

The college essay plays a special role in American higher education. The American system, more so than higher education in most countries, encourages a student's self-directed development. Writing essays in which you say what you think and why is crucial to that development. Writing an essay means working within a rigid framework of formats and conventions, but it requires much more than technique; in a college essay, the personal qualities of its author, passionate as well as rational, take center stage.

An essay, like a personality, hangs together through a delicate balance of forces; it should be clear but not empty, thoughtful but down-to-earth, strong-minded but fair-minded. The writer must be adept at making arguments and synthesizing and analyzing others' ideas, but original and honest. A good essay is a small piece of one's better self—more rational, more critical, and more cogent than one is in everyday speech or idle thought, yet also more spirited. When you write an essay you enter into the most challenging yet rewarding of the liberal arts: shaping your ideas, questions, and convictions to share with others.

For all that, an essay is written on paper, not carved in stone. Essays are, in the root sense of the word, tries. *To essay* originally meant to attempt or put to the test (and still does, in *assay* and the French *essayer*). The essay as a literary form became popular at the beginning of the modern scientific age, part of a seismic cultural shift away from received wisdom and toward inquiry and exploration. (Montaigne's

celebrated essays, genial and ruminative, helped establish the genre's
tone in the latter half of the sixteenth century.) The essay has flourished
ever since, as men and women have claimed increasing space to think
for themselves. Essays, imbued with the spirit of inquiry, put ideas and
assumptions to the test, and if they sometimes stumble or equivocate,
that is part of their nature (Samuel Johnson's eighteenth-century dictionary defined an essay as "a loose sally of the mind; an irregular indi-
gested piece"). The writer of an essay is a kind of intellectual entrepreneur,
taking a risk to say something new.

But college essays are written in an environment in many ways ill
suited to risk taking. The solemn trappings of college culture—degrees,
grades, academic titles—can make it seem that formality is the most
important thing to aim at. It's natural for many students to think that their
goal is to learn what their professors know, or think what their professors
think. Every area of study from anthropology to zoology has its own
jargon and its own rules about what to study, how to study it, and how
to write up one's ideas and explorations. And when students start reading academic writing, what they typically see doesn't seem to include
much room for risk taking: formality, a more serious tone than students
have encountered before, and hard-won familiarity with "the literature," that daunting mountain of published scholarship in every academic
discipline.

The most successful writing in this academic environment is dense
with learning. Here are two examples of good writing by respected
scholars. Both examples display full-throated academic voices, each of
them a striking blend of expert scholarship and sure-footed expression:

Like so many of the key ideas in Weber's sociology—*verstehen*, legitimacy, inner-worldly asceticism, rationalization—the concept of charisma
suffers from an uncertainty of referent: does it denote a cultural phenomenon or a psychological one? At once "a certain quality" that marks an
individual as standing in a privileged relationship to the sources of being
and a hypnotic power "certain personalities" have to engage passions and
dominate minds, it is not clear whether charisma is the status, the excite-
ment, or some ambiguous fusion of the two. The attempt to write a sociology of culture and a social psychology in a single set of sentences is what
gives Weber's work its orchestral complexity and harmonic depth. But
it is also what gives it, especially to ears less attuned to polyphony, its

chronic elusiveness. (Clifford Geertz, *Local Knowledge: Further Essays in Interpretive Anthropology*)

The doctrine of Purgatory, as we have seen, occupied a place at the center of Christendom's ritualized strategies of familiarity, containment, and control. These strategies extended to the precise calculation of the number of masses or quantity of alms that might be required in relation to the probable number of years of purgatorial suffering, an "accounting of the hereafter" that Jacques Chiffoleau has related to the rise in the later Middle Ages of double-entry bookkeeping. By these means, the living no longer need to feel paralyzed with anxiety and uncertainty in the face of spectral visitations. (Stephen Greenblatt, *Hamlet in Purgatory*)

Confronted every day with such nearly majestic writing, a student is anxiously aware of how little, by comparison, she knows, and how less impressive is her own writing. No wonder, then, that when a temptation to appear learned squares off against a habit of using plain English, temptation usually wins. Here, for instance, is a sentence from a student's scholarship-application essay:

Reflecting back and providing insight on what I gained from my four years in the system, I hopefully have allowed a plethora of new concepts and perhaps even new educational-administrative philosophies to surface.

This student is trying furiously to write like a scholar. The passages from Geertz and Greenblatt use big words sensibly, as the best way to convey the authors' complex and sharply observed arguments; the student's passage uses big words merely to dress up a simple—though sensible and indeed powerful—point. Why? The student is afraid he will seem simpleminded if he says something as plain as this:

In my four years of high school, I've learned a lot about how schools work and how students learn.

But this is not simpleminded at all—rather, it is simple, and far more powerful than the first version (once we get past the dazzle of all those big words).

The aim of this book is to convince you that plain, direct writing is the most effective way to express your ideas, even in college. Plainness makes it easier to spot your argument and harder to hide behind words. But simplicity is not necessarily easy. Indeed, this book will complicate writing for you by suggesting a number of things to think about as you write. But the effort will be worthwhile. Mastering a plain, clear style is an indispensable step in one's education. You're not in college to imitate the erudition of your professors or even to learn their opinions, but to develop your capacity for independent critical thinking and judgment. As you learn more you'll find yourself with more to say, and you'll make increasingly sophisticated and nuanced arguments—but always building on a foundation of clear expression.

Learning to distinguish between clear and unclear writing will also help you understand what you read, both in college and elsewhere. Professional writing—memos, contracts, public documents, and the like—often seems intended to impede rather than promote understanding. ("A memorandum," former secretary of state Dean Acheson once observed, "is written not to inform the reader but to protect the writer.") Nowadays a company is likely to call a loss "negative earnings"; bolder companies issue "pro forma" financial statements, a little Latin phrase that in effect lets them make up their own rules about what and how to count financial results. But deceptive language is not limited to the commercial sphere. Public broadcasting stations, of course, can't have ads; instead, "enhanced underwriting" lets "underwriters" (not advertisers) buy airtime on PBS shows. Former Fed chairman Alan Greenspan, an experienced political figure whose slightest word could move markets, was famous for his opaque and Delphic style (after the Greek oracle whose predictions were often conveniently ambiguous). Chairman Greenspan would never bluntly call a recession a recession; the closest he would come would be a blurry phrase like "significant cyclical adjustment."

George Orwell, the English novelist and essayist, said more than sixty years ago that insincere language was the curse of the modern age. Politicians, Orwell said, feared to speak the blunt truth to citizens, while even in democracies citizens failed to demand truth from their leaders. Orwell's word for duplicitous language has entered the English language: "doublespeak." In Orwell's great novel *1984* the propaganda ministry—in charge of all the government's lying—is called the Ministry of Truth. In his allegory *Animal Farm* an animal paradise turns into a dictatorship as the cleverest animals, the pigs, take over, justifying their power grab with an immortal formulation: "All animals are equal—but some are more equal than others." Both stories pose in sharpest form the basic question of how we use language—to tell the truth as we see it, or to hide behind words. In a classic essay, "Politics and the English Language," Orwell said that the renewal of politics and language would begin with the choices of ordinary people like you and me about how to speak and write: "If you simplify your English," he challenges his reader, ". . . when you make a stupid remark its stupidity will be obvious, even to yourself" (1968, 139).

But unfortunately the trends Orwell saw in the 1940s have, if anything, strengthened. In politics, at work, at school we swim in a sea of doublespeak. Any half-decent politician or lawyer today can spew forth obfuscatory words "like a cuttlefish squirting out ink," as Orwell put it (1968, 137). Enron, the poster child of 1990s corporate fraud, for years filed numbingly long financial statements full of obscure terms like "special purpose entities." It was a strategy of deliberate opacity that let the company hide its fraud in plain sight, as it were (confused stock analysts mainly stayed mum for fear they'd be laughed out of their jobs if they admitted they didn't understand Enron's statements).[1] Today attorneys learn to speak in a camouflaged manner almost by reflex, as part of defending their clients. An attorney for Enron, for instance, fended off an accusation of misconduct on his client's part: "I am unaware of any evidence that supports the allegation there was improper selling by members of the board or senior management" (CNN Newsroom). Such verbiage—windy, vague, almost automatically evasive—has been called a variety of things. Orwell called it the "inflated style" (1968, 136). Richard Lanham labels it the "official style." I call it the pompous style.

Of course, not all grand and ornate writing is deceptive or unclear. Many great scholars, like the eighteenth-century historian Edward Gibbon, write prose that is complex and dense, yet famously clear. And passages like those of Geertz and Greenblatt quoted above possess clarity as well as power and dignity. Done properly, grand writing can be

---

1. Finance may be especially prone to obfuscation. A 2019 paper by three economists examined mortgage-backed securities, which played a key role in the financial crisis of 2007–2009. They found that more complex securities—measured by variables like number of pages in the prospectus, number of tranches (pieces of separate mortgages bundled together), and number of different types of collateral—defaulted at a higher rate, had more foreclosures, and provided a lower return than less complex securities. But more complex and hard-to-understand securities received higher grades from credit-rating companies! The lesson, even from the hard-bitten world of financial professionals staking real money on their ability to read and understand, is that obfuscation can be a winning strategy—at least for the obfuscators, and at least until something terrible happens. See Ghent et al., 2019.

wondrously effective. But it is not generally a style that suits undergraduate college students. For most, adopting a sturdy, direct, plain style is a better choice. Learn to write plainly, and you will more likely write clearly as you take on deeper subjects and become a better stylist.

The pompous style muffles and depersonalizes action. It cloaks itself in the language of science, hoping to take on a sense of scientific objectivity and credibility. No police officer, for instance, would ever report, "I put him in a headlock." Instead he would say, "The suspect was restrained." A government agency like the Fish and Wildlife Service prefers the cool term "taking" to plainly saying that some animals die as a result of its policies; and it prefers the technical sound of "lethal control" to the bluntness of "sometimes we have to go out and shoot wolves that are killing livestock."

Death, especially the killing of human beings, tends to bring forth the most strenuous applications of the pompous style. A politician answers accusations of long-ago war crimes when he was a soldier with the bland statement that the platoon he led "used lethal methods" (not only is the phrasing antiseptic; it evades the question of who was killed). An American military official, responding to concern about civilian deaths from NATO bombing in Kosovo in 1999, responds as inertly as possible: "the collateral damage which has been done by NATO is at an absolute minimum, and we take great care in both targeting and in terms of the application of fire power to ensure that collateral damage does not occur" ("Pentagon Briefing"). The statement was not a lie but a practiced use of generalities and abstractions intended to lead the listener's mind away from the specific and concrete—men, women, and children killed by errant NATO bombs. As Orwell pointed out more than a half century ago, this is the chief educated idiom of our time: "The whole tendency of modern prose is away from concreteness" (1968, 133).

The tendency toward abstraction reaches every corner of society, but is especially common in public and academic settings. All of us shift discursive styles when we move from private to public settings—the next time you see ordinary people interviewed on TV after something newsworthy has happened in their neighborhood, listen to the formal and stilted way most of them speak in front of the camera. Sudden shifts between the pompous and plain styles can make us smile, as when a TV announcer explained why a football player had been thrown out of a game: "Jay Leeuwenberg was the recipient of his anger. That means that's the guy he kicked."

To be sure, various degrees of formality are appropriate in various kinds of academic writing, and it's hard to write (or indeed think) about ideas without using abstractions. But none of this requires pomposity. So accustomed are we to the pompous style as the voice of authority that students can't be blamed for thinking it the way they should write in school. Indeed our educational institutions—ahem, schools—do much to encourage this belief. Children learn to read and write short, plain sentences—"See Spot run"—then grow older and begin to write as if "Observe Spot in the process of running" were somehow an improvement. By the time they arrive at college, almost all revere formality in and of itself as the mark of good writing. And by and large they learn to write like George Eliot's self-important man of business, Borthrop Trumbull, talked: "Things never began with Mr. Trumbull: they always commenced."

The Borthrop Trumbulls of this world, successful and stuck in their ways, may be a lost cause. But in the following pages I'm going to try to change *your* mind, at least, about the use and abuse of written English. This book will help you develop a sound college writing style, a style that combines the essential elements of academic convention with clear expression. It will show you how to make your writing clearer and more precise by developing a style whose hallmarks are plain words, active verbs, and uncluttered syntax. We'll begin with concision and clarity, emphasizing the importance of verbs. Then we'll consider how to give writing a sense of flow, how to punctuate effectively, and how to make your writing more graceful. Next comes a chapter on sources. In the final two chapters we'll move to larger structural elements, with thoughts on paragraphs and the beginnings and endings of essays. At the end there's an appendix on common document and citation formats (CMOS, MLA, and APA), but our main aim is showing you how clarity and plainness can make you a better writer and a clearer thinker. Let's ~~commence~~ begin.

1 Concision

CONCISION, THE LEANNESS or lack of fat in a piece of writing, is a natural place to begin because wordiness is so common in student writing and because (unlike losing weight), writing concisely isn't really so hard. It usually works by process of elimination: we watch what we say, ask ourselves whether what we've said is essential to what we mean, and eliminate what isn't. The real work is often figuring out what exactly we wanted to say in the first place. But trying to be concise helps with that too—by helping us see what we don't mean.

Concision can add remarkable grace to our prose. It also makes our prose easier to read and understand. Yet many of us are afraid of writing concisely because doing so can make us feel exposed. Concision leaves us fewer words to hide behind. Our insights and ideas might appear puny stripped of those inessential words, phrases, and sentences in which we rough them out. We might even wonder, were we to cut out the fat, would anything be left? It's no wonder, then, that many students make little attempt to be concise—may, in fact, go out of their way not to be—and so often couple this strategy with a style just as mistaken. Though you can certainly be wordy without writing pompously—and the other way around—the two go hand in hand so often that it's useful to consider them together. Here's how lots of students think they have to write in college:

> Prospero is faced with the necessity of deciding whether to accept forgiveness for the actions of his brother or remain in a state of hostility.

> It is evident that interpersonal conflict is responsible for many organizational problems experienced by businesses.

> The role of women in households in medieval Europe was arrayed across a number of possibilities of increasing or decreasing activity and independence, depending on variables such as status, wealth, religion, or region.

That's the collegiate pompous style in action: big words, self-important phrasing, a flat tone, long gobs of prepositional phrases, nouns galore, and abuse of the passive voice—all of it run up the flag pole to see if the powers that be will salute.

The pompous style spreads like crabgrass, and can be as hard to root out. Here's a legal sentence crafted in classic pompous style, from Maryland's *Annotated Code of Laws*:

> Any investigation, inquiry, hearing, or examination which the Board is empowered by law to hold or undertake may be held or undertaken by or before the majority of the members of the Board or its secretary, and the finding or order of members of the Board or the representative, when concurred in by the majority of the members of the Board, shall have the same force and effect as the finding or order of the whole Board (Article 56, Section 497). (77 words)

This sentence is a parade of legalese. And even if we don't understand it, its gassiness is almost reassuring—this is what we've come to expect "the law" to sound and feel like. But here's the same code, revised when the state, in a temporary fit of sanity, decided to make its laws intelligible to ordinary people (Hackett B1):

> A majority of the members then serving on the Board is a quorum. (13 words)

The result is an 83 percent reduction in length. It took courage to get rid of those twenty-dollar words like *empowered, finding*, and *concurred*. But now we have a sentence that is much easier to read. It sounds strange to us, perhaps—aren't laws supposed to sound like, well, laws? But if one imagines the thousands of laws, the book upon book of legal code, that could be simplified and compressed, one is likely to agree that from a citizen's perspective this is a vast improvement. (It is not incidental that the most enduring laws in Western culture, the Ten Commandments, are expressed in a succinct, lapidary style.)

Here's another example, from a different professional setting but with no less pomposity. This is a technical manual for programmers revising a corporate computer system:

> To ensure that the new system being developed, or the existing system being modified, will provide users with the timely, accurate, and complete information they require to properly perform their functions and responsibilities, it is necessary to assure that the new or modified system will

cover all necessary aspects of the present automated or manual systems being replaced. To gain this assurance, it is essential that documentation be made of the entities of the present systems which will be modified or eliminated. (82 words)

This passage displays the same faults as the legal sentence. Its writer tries to convey its importance by stamping pretentious words all over it and piling on the verbiage. But the passage lulls the reader to sleep and thus defeats the point of writing in the first place. Bold pruning yields this core meaning:

> Make sure to document all planned changes so any mistakes you make can be corrected. (15 words)

Another 80 percent reduction in length. As with the legal sentence, the revision may sound less important (though that *mistakes you make* might catch the attention of those programmers who hold the future of the company in their hands). But it has lost not a shred of meaning. (That might be easier to see if we keep in mind that this instruction would occur in the context of a wider discussion of the computer system and planned changes.) If you're not sure the revision is really an improvement, consider what it would be like to read through page after page of the original. You'd go to sleep. Now conduct the same thought experiment with the revision, and ask yourself which version you'd rather read.

The Pompous Style at School

College students begin their training in the pompous style innocently enough, with sentences like this:

> To satisfy her hunger for nutrition, she ate the bread.

Once you've decided to write in a formal tone, stilted phrases like *hunger for nutrition* arise almost automatically. But the sentence's tone is just too weighty for its message. Simplifying makes the sentence shorter and stronger:

> She was hungry, so she ate the bread.

In the following instances, see if you can figure out what gets changed or cut to go from pompous or wordy prose to plain prose:

Pompous or Wordy Original	Plain Revision
It was discussed in this reading that . . .	Tannen argues that . . .
The scene is very important because it helps us understand Cleopatra early on in the play.	This early scene helps us understand Cleopatra.
In the play, Menas, who is a pirate, says this about the marriage: "I think the policy of that purpose made more in the marriage than the love of the parties" (2.6.115–16).	The pirate Menas dismisses the marriage as a political arrangement.
The film and video industry category can specifically be broken down into subsequent industries of motion picture and videotape production, motion picture and videotape distribution, movie houses, and cable and other pay-television services.	The film and video industry category consists of production, distribution, theaters, and cable and other pay-television services.
Some of AT&T's major media competitors include Comcast Corporation, which is a global media and entertainment media power located in Philadelphia, and Viacom Inc., which is based in New York and is one of the world's leading media companies.	AT&T's major global media competitors include Comcast and Viacom.

Do you see any patterns in the revisions? There's a hefty reduction in the total number of words. About 70 percent of the words in the original passages have been eliminated. But how does one decide what to cut? Here are some of the structural changes that make these revisions more concise: the verbs have gotten stronger (fewer linking verbs and less passive voice, and more active verbs in the active voice); adjective phrases and clauses have been pushed into short adjectives that precede nouns;

some adverbs have been cut; repetitive words and phrases have been squeezed together with tricks like parallelism; and a difficult quotation has been paraphrased. These structural changes have moved the writing away from the pompous style and toward a more concise, vigorous, verb-centered style.

Later we'll look closer at some of these techniques. For now, let's focus on gaining the skill and confidence to pluck out empty modifiers. The pompous style prefers description over action, so it bristles with adjectives and adverbs. A useful step in unlearning the pompous style is to hunt for modifiers that add little or nothing:

Original	Revision
Women held an important place in ~~social~~ society.	Women held an important place in society.
Capitalism is accompanied by the ideal of freedom ~~as some- thing to be attained~~.	Capitalism is accompanied by the ideal of freedom.

An *ideal* is, by definition, *something to be attained*.

But sometimes a student resists cutting empty words because they seem to add important information. What do you think about the following cut?

Original	Revision
~~From a political-institutional point of view,~~ the Federalist Papers were the first full formulation of feder-alism as a theory.	The Federalist Papers were the first full formulation of federalism as a theory.

Political-institutional is the kind of claptrap that makes the pompous style so tempting for inexperienced writers. It sounds weighty but adds nothing. The "point of view," whatever that means here, is obvious from the content of the sentence—especially if we remember that this sentence will be read in its context, as part of an exploration of the topic.

Another example:

Original	Revision
These are the practical ~~contin- gency management~~ implications:	These are the practical implications:

If we imagine the context, plainly this sentence occurs within a larger discussion in which the topic, *contingency management,* has already been introduced (otherwise the use of the phrase in this sentence would make no sense). The topic's repetition here blunts the energy of a sturdy little sentence.

When a student is wise enough to use a good verb, intensifying adverbs often backfire:

Original	Revision
Euthyphro continues to ~~further~~ justify his actions.	Euthyphro continues to justify his actions.
The play ~~carefully~~ examines the disorder brought by civil war.	The play examines the disorder brought by civil war.

These adverbs add nothing to the already strong verbs. They are just traces of the pompous style in otherwise good sentences. Keep in mind Mark Twain's advice: "Substitute *damn* every time you're inclined to write *very*; your editor will delete it and the writing will be just as it should be."

Since adverbs often prop up weak verbs, sometimes cutting an adverb will push the writer to choose a stronger verb:

Original	Revision
Antony plays on the crowd's emotions and successfully obtains their support.	Antony plays on the crowd's emotions and wins their support.

Here the writer, trying to fix the problem of an unhelpful modifier, realized that the solution was to put the sentence's key action into its verb:

Original	Revision
Socrates convincingly explains his position to Crito.	Socrates convinces Crito that it would be unjust to flee. / Eventually, Socrates convinces Crito.

Socrates convinces Crito by itself would be a bit abrupt, so the writer's next step was to decide how to add enough value to the sentence to make it read well. Two possibilities are shown.

Wordiness, as we've seen, is often tied to other problems, and the effort to make one's writing concise often brings about other improvements. Consider this opening paragraph of a student essay about the Italian Renaissance political thinker Machiavelli:

> Machiavelli best supports republics in *The Discourses*. His favorite republic is ancient Rome. He explains and supports his admiration in this work. The two major aspects that Machiavelli discusses are that the Romans were a great empire and that they had a powerful army. (44 words)

Right away the reader stumbles over *best supports*. What does it mean to say that Machiavelli supports republics? And why say *best*, a word that implies a comparison? As is often true of unclear writing, its writer has good ideas but hasn't yet succeeded in articulating them. The first of these is that Machiavelli praises republics in a book entitled *The Discourses*. The revision will build on this plainer verb, *praises*. The writer's second idea, only hinted at in that distracting word *best*, is that Machiavelli's praise of republics in *The Discourses* differs from his perspective in his other famous book, *The Prince*, where he seems to prefer monarchies. (We'd only know this in context, so to speak—if we were along for the ride with that student—but bear with me.) Mulling over ways to bring out this second point, the writer realizes she can skip it because it's not the point of her essay:

Original	Revision 1	Revision 2
Machiavelli best supports republics in *The Discourses*.	Machiavelli best praises republics in *The Discourses*.	Machiavelli praises republics in *The Discourses*.

There's still work to do. Look back at the original paragraph. The transitions between sentences are weak, and the third sentence adds little to the first. Here's the revised paragraph:

> Machiavelli praises republics in *The Discourses*. Above all he praises the Roman republic, because it had a powerful army, and conquered and held a vast empire. (26 words)

The revision is 40 percent shorter. It keeps the same ideas (except for cutting the abortive contrast with *The Prince*) but expresses them with strong verbs (*praises, had, conquered*, and *held*) and good links (*Above all* and *because*).

Finally, note that the revision orders and expands the argument. The original version listed as *major aspects* (whatever that means) that Rome was an empire and had a strong army. The revision reverses the order of these items, since a strong army is what allowed Rome to gain its empire. And while the original says merely that the Romans *were* a great empire, the revision turns this identity into actions, *conquered* and *held*.

Here's a student trying to cram too many ideas into too small a space:

> *Alien 3* is a fast-paced, emotionally tense film composed of a vast array of symbols and meanings which reflect the political debates concerning women's reproductive rights in 1990s America. (29 words)

The idea is a good one, but the sentence, running without a pause, is too long for easy reading (pauses help readers make it through long sentences). And some of the verbiage veers into pomposity—a windy, hackneyed phrase like *vast array* should be a red flag. The solution is to cut to the core of the argument:

> *Alien 3* is a powerful allegory of the 1990s American debate about women's reproductive rights. (15 words)

The revision is half as long. Note how the windy *composed of a vast array of symbols and meanings* is captured and even sharpened in a single well-chosen word, *allegory*. *Emotionally tense* comes from the same pompous-style tendency: tension *is* emotional by definition, so *emotionally tense* is redundant. *Powerful*, the revision's choice of adjective, is vaguer and broader than *fast-paced* and *tense*, but that's a good choice here, where we want to focus the reader's attention on that key word *allegory*.

Note the mock profundity of this example from a marketing paper:

> The company uses specific determination methods to make distinctions between customer segments. (12 words)

Specific, as used above, is a favorite pompous-style word, a vague term masquerading as a concrete one. And the gassy *uses specific determination methods to make distinctions* can be compressed into one word:

The company distinguishes between customer segments.

This is much better, but the revision isn't complete. It feels bare and overly general. The writer should provide more information to make the sentence feel full enough:

The company distinguishes between three customer segments. (7 words)

That's more like it. The sentence goes from vapid to informative—a good lesson that concision is more than many words versus few, or long versus short. Here, as so often, the challenge to be concise compels the writer to say something concrete and informative.

Now let's look at a sentence that replaces a typical pompous-style verb-swaddle with a strong verb:

Original	Revision
This secrecy becomes very damaging to Hamlet.	This secrecy cripples Hamlet.

Many students are uneasy with changes of this kind. They seem too bold. *Becomes very damaging* has a safe clinical sound, while *cripples* sounds almost rude to students schooled in the pompous style. But for anyone with an ear for English, the revision is better. It can stand by itself or serve as a frame on which to add nuance:

This secrecy cripples Hamlet by destroying his ability to trust.

Some may protest that this kind of revision changes the meaning. I would answer that the original sentence had *already* changed the meaning—it took what was a good idea on the writer's part, and sucked the life out of it.

Concision, to sum up, may start out simple—cut the fat!—but it becomes more complicated as we work deeper into our prose. Concision represents a careful, patient process of revision in which we weigh every word and phrase and think hard about how we can better develop, organize, articulate, and refine our ideas. Most writers produce wordy first drafts. Good writers realize that sad fact and are willing to spend time tightening their prose. Concision, in other words, is more a sign of perspiration than inspiration. As Pascal wrote in 1656, "This letter is long because I didn't have time to make it shorter."

2 Clarity

MOST OF US think our writing is clearer than it really is. We know what we mean, so we see it in what we write. But good writers see their words from the reader's perspective, because clarity, like beauty, is in the eye of the beholder. Good writers ask, "Does my reader understand the words I'm using, in the way I'm using them? Have I explained enough so that she knows what I'm talking about? Is my evidence persuasive? Have I thought about possible objections? Is there a logical arrangement to my argument that will help the reader follow it? Have I used good links and transitions to keep her pointed in the right direction?"

One problem in answering these questions is that readers differ, so there's no one standard of clear writing. A general audience, for instance, needs more background and explanation than a scholarly one. Unless you know your audience, it's impossible to be assured that what you're writing will be well-received. Most undergraduate essays should be aimed at an audience of one's better classmates unless a teacher says otherwise. Such a standard will help you decide how much to explain, what terms to define, and what tone to strike: competent, disciplined plainness.

People tend to perceive a sentence as clear when its "narrative"—generally, the story it tells or the relationship it describes—corresponds to its grammatical structure. In other words, if you wish to write clearly, begin by making your narrative's characters the subjects of sentences, and their actions and identities the predicates. Some examples:

This process is called continental drift. Over time it has reshaped the surface of the earth.

Lavoisier gave Priestley's "dephlogisticated air" its modern scientific name, oxygen.

On December 11, 2001, China formally joined the World Trade Organization.

Early in his career Shakespeare wrote two narrative poems.

Historically, most patriarchies have institutionalized force through their legal systems. (Kate Millett, *Sexual Politics*)

The basic pattern is *who* (or *what*) *does what*. Logical actors like *Lavoisier, China, Shakespeare*, and *patriarchies* are made grammatical subjects. (In the first example a pronoun, *it*, points back to *continental drift*.) Actions—*reshaped, gave, joined, wrote, have institutionalized*—are expressed as verbs. These sentences are clear because their grammar matches their narrative.

When a writer doesn't do this the result is likely to strike us as confusing—and sometimes even comical, as in this passage from an accident report filed with an insurance company:

The telephone pole was approaching. I was attempting to swerve out of its way, when it struck my front end.

Trying to find something else to blame for his one-car accident, the writer gives the telephone pole a life of its own. How? By making it the grammatical subject of two active verbs, *was approaching* and *struck*. Note that you can't chalk this up to lack of skill, but to a clever, if unsuccessful, attempt to hide behind words.

The question of *who did what* is known as agency. We tend to express ourselves clearly when agency is reflected in grammar: that is, when we express agents as subjects of sentences. Muddying up the question of agency is the root cause of most unclear student writing. Consider this passage from an essay about a court case:

A motion was requested by the defendant for the case to be dismissed on the grounds that there was a failure on the part of the prosecution to establish the facts. This was accepted by the judge, and dismissal of the case was ordered. (44 words)

True, the passage describes actions and identifies the actors. But its clunky design makes it hard to figure out who's doing what. Here's a clearer revision:

The defendant moved to dismiss the case on the grounds that the prosecution had not established the facts. The judge agreed and dismissed the case. (25 words)

The revision is about 40 percent shorter.

who	the defendant	the prosecution	the judge
did	filed	had not established	agreed and dismissed
what	a motion	facts	the case

To answer the question *Who did what?* you'd have to take apart the original and rearrange its pieces. The grammar of the revision, by contrast, makes answering this question a breeze. The revision shows three techniques for achieving greater clarity: (1) choose verbs over nominalizations, (2) choose active verbs over linking verbs, and (3) choose the active voice over the passive voice (see Diagram 1 for help with these terms).

Active Voice
The subject performs the action.
I threw the ball.
Bill Gates founded Microsoft.
The president made a mistake.

Passive Voice
The subject receives the action.
The ball was thrown.
Microsoft was founded in 1975.
Mistakes were made.

Voice
A property of transitive verbs. Refers to how
you express action with the verb—with the subject
performing the action or **receiving** the action.

Transitive Verbs
Express action on a direct object.
The dog bit me.
She appealed the decision.
I dropped my backpack.

Intransitive Verbs
Express action without a direct object.
Rain poured through the open window.
The experiment failed.
The backpack dropped in the mud.

Active Verbs
Express an action of some kind.
She hurried to catch up.
He felt raindrops.
The Incas ruled a large empire.

Linking Verbs
Express a state of being or identity.
The experiment was a failure.
Hamlet feels alienated.
Results look promising.

Verbs

Diagram 1. A Verb Family Tree

None of these techniques should be considered an absolute rule. There are many times a good writer uses nominalizations, linking verbs, and the passive voice. But since those three elements constitute the structural core of the pompous style, and are habitually overused by college students, it's best to view them skeptically and know how to avoid them.

Choose Verbs over Nominalizations

A nominalization is an action expressed as a noun rather than a verb, like *analysis* or *assessment* rather than *analyze* or *assess* (some words in English, especially short words like *talk* or *work*, look the same as verbs and nouns; it's their function that counts). Nominalizations often end in *-tion* or *-ion*:

Verb	Nominalization		Verb	Nominalization
act	action		examine	examination
analyze	analysis		explain	explanation
argue	argument		fail	failure
behave	behavior		investigate	investigation
describe	description		nominalize	nominalization
dismiss	dismissal		perform	performance
distort	distortion		reveal, show	revelation

The common *-ion* endings make it easy to find nominalizations in writing, and once you start looking for them you'll find a lot, especially in formal writing—as H. W. Fowler lamented years ago:

> Turgid flabby English is full of abstract nouns; the commonest ending of abstract nouns is *-tion*, and to count the *-ion* words in what one has written . . . is one of the simplest and most effective means of making oneself less unreadable. (640)

By changing actions into nouns, nominalizations let you write sentences that don't make clear *who does what*. "Analysis," for instance, doesn't specify who's doing the analyzing. Sometimes that's okay. Consider the following:

Action in Verb	Action in Nominalization
I **did** all I could.	A full complement of **actions** was undertaken
We **are** carefully **analyzing** the data.	A systematic **analysis** of the data is underway.

In sentences like these, which report on the scientific method, nominalizations (and their partner the passive voice) are commonly—and sensibly—used, because there is no real doubt about who is doing the actions (scientists write up their own findings). But when agency is uncertain, then nominalizations tend to make prose seem confusing or clunky, as in the following examples:

Nominalized Original	Clearer Revision
The play is an examination of the conflict the conspirators face after the assassination of Julius Caesar.	The play examines the conflict the conspirators face after they assassinate Julius Caesar.
The love Antony has for Cleopatra is much greater than any love he has for his wife.	Antony loves Cleopatra more than he loves his wife.
Assessment of his test performance showed satisfactory achievement.	He passed the test.

Another example:

Nominalized Original	Clearer Revision
Today, society witnesses the steady progress of women toward equality with their increasing presence in the working world and in government and their gradual move outside the home.	Today, society witnesses women's steady progress toward equality. Moving beyond the limits of the home, women are claiming new and increasing authority in government, business, and other traditionally male-dominated areas.

This revision divides the long string of words into two sentences, which already makes it easier to follow. It also aligns the character with the grammatical subject, by making *women* the subject of the verb in the second sentence. True, the revision is longer, but its new readability more than makes up for the added length. Concision isn't an end in itself, but a means to clarity.

Choose Active Verbs over Linking Verbs

Not all verbs work the same way. Active verbs convey action—*he ran, she spoke, the patient suffered a relapse.* Linking verbs convey states of being or description—*my friend is in London, she seems smart, it will be difficult.*[1] It's natural to use linking verbs when you're defining or describing things:

> According to Kübler-Ross there are five stages of grief or dying.

> Poland's Solidarity was the first independent trade union in the Soviet bloc.

> Machiavelli's cynicism seems utterly contemporary.

So far so good. But when this grammar of identity is used to convey actions, things get ugly. When Bill Clinton was being sued for sexual harassment by Paula Jones, his attorney told the judge in the case that the president knew of an affidavit (false, as it turned out) by Monica Lewinsky, which affirmed, as the attorney put it, that "there is absolutely no sex of any kind" with the president. The linking-verb construction might sound clumsy, but it cleverly treated *sex* impersonally. The attorney— clearly a master of the pompous style—did all he could to avoid conjuring any image of the president *in flagrante delicto.* The inert linking verb also finessed the issue of timing (past or present?). President Clinton later tried to rebut an accusation of perjury by hiding behind the vagueness of this particular linking verb: "It depends on what the meaning of the word 'is' is" ("The President's Testimony" B3).

That's a notorious example from sworn testimony, but linking-verb constructions make it all too easy to obscure actions in everyday speech. If the action isn't in its natural place—the verb—where is it? As you

---

1. The forms of *to be* in statements like *she was running* or *my friend is studying in London* are not linking verbs, but auxiliaries that are part of compound verbs (the other part is a participle: the *-ing* forms here are present participles).

probably suspect, in a nominalization. Linking verbs and nominalizations occur together as elements of the pompous style, so replacing them in tandem tends to result in more dynamic sentences:

Linking-Verb Original	Active-Verb Revision
A mood of ambivalence is the main effect of the poem's language and imagery.	The poem's language and imagery evoke a mood of ambivalence.
Motion toward a light source is a behavior of *Euglena*, a single-celled organism.	*Euglena*, a single-celled organism, will move toward a light source.
There was a failure on the part of the accounting firm to engage in a thorough examination of the transactions of the company.	The accounting firm failed to examine the company's transactions carefully.

The third example shows a common trait of linking-verb sentences—a chain of prepositional phrases that makes for a plodding, monotonous rhythm:

> There was a failure
>   on the part
>   of the accounting firm
>   to engage
>   in a thorough examination
>   of the transactions
>   of the company.

Since the pompous style prefers nouns to verbs, it tends to overuse the prepositional phrase, that handy device for stapling nouns into sentences. When you build sentences on active verbs rather than nominalizations and linking verbs, you'll use fewer prepositional phrases. Now let's turn to the third technique for writing clearly.

Choose the Active Voice over the Passive Voice

Sentences written in the passive voice turn the usual narrative pattern upside down. The subject doesn't do anything—it is acted upon: *A car was stolen.* The doer of the action often drops out altogether. Before looking at abuses of the passive voice, consider some examples that make good use of it:

> The document was found in the governor's personal library.
>
> *Hamlet* was written around 1600.
>
> The particle's rate of decay was measured.

In all three of these sentences the passive voice works well (though to decide for sure we'd want to see the context and know the writer's intention). In general, the passive voice makes sense when you want to emphasize an action or its recipient and don't care about the agent. If you do want to identify the agent in the passive voice, use a prepositional phrase beginning with *by*: *Hamlet was written by Shakespeare around 1600.*

You can also use the passive voice to give a sentence more pizzazz by identifying the agent at the end of the sentence. In the following two-sentence sequence, for instance, the writer uses the active voice and then the passive, according to his purpose in each sentence:

> Horses, mammoths, reindeer, bison, mountain goats, lions, and a host of other mammals cascade in image along the cave walls over a distance of almost a hundred yards, over three hundred depictions in all. Delicately executed and meticulously observed, these varied and overlapping images were made by people of the late Ice Age, perhaps thirteen thousand years ago. (Ian Tattersall, *Becoming Human*)

The first sentence, with its active voice and strong verb (*cascade*), emphasizes the lively energy of the paintings. The second sentence uses the passive voice and a *by* phrase to identify the agent at the end. That lets the second sentence start where the first leaves off. If the second sentence were recast in the active voice—say, *People of the late Ice Age made these varied and overlapping images, perhaps thirteen thousand years ago*—the passage would lose much of its interest (though none of its meaning).

A classic use of the passive voice comes from President Franklin Delano Roosevelt's address to Congress the day after the Japanese attack on Pearl Harbor:

Yesterday, December 7, 1941—a date which will live in infamy—the United States of America was suddenly and deliberately attacked by naval and air forces of the Empire of Japan.

Why the passive voice here? To reinforce FDR's argument that America had done nothing to provoke the attack. Later, the president uses the active voice in a strong parallel series to emphasize Japan's active perfidy:

Yesterday, the Japanese government also launched an attack against Malaya. Last night, Japanese forces attacked Hong Kong.
Last night, Japanese forces attacked Guam.
Last night, Japanese forces attacked the Philippine Islands. Last night, the Japanese attacked Wake Island.
This morning, the Japanese attacked Midway Island.

At the end, not wanting to leave his listeners with a message of their country's passivity, Roosevelt again uses the active voice—this time to assert America's unbroken resolve: "The American people in their righteous might will win through to absolute victory."

In sum, when Roosevelt wanted to emphasize innocence he used the passive voice. When he wanted to emphasize action he used the active voice. His masterly use of voice is the essence of good style: when *how* we say something suits *what* we say.

Here's another great example of how to use the passive voice to make a sentence more powerful. In a December 2004 speech, Dubai's crown prince deftly juxtaposed active voice and passive voice to add rhetorical oomph to his call for political reform:

I say to my fellow Arabs in charge: If you do not change, you will be changed.

As these examples show, the passive voice has its uses. But most of the time when good writers tell, describe, or explore, they reach for the active voice. If the passive voice dominates someone's style, it's a fair assumption that he or she is more interested in obscuring or ducking questions of responsibility than in frank expression. Indeed, politicians and others eager to appear contrite without actually taking responsibility cherish one particular passive construction: *Mistakes were made.* Here are some prizewinners:

Deng: Why is there still such a big noise being made about Watergate? Kissinger: That is a series of almost incomprehensible events. . . . It has its roots in the fact that some mistakes were made, but also, when you change many policies, you make many, many enemies.

Secretary of State Henry Kissinger speaking
with Chinese Vice Premier Deng Xiaoping
(April 14, 1974)

The execution of these policies was flawed and mistakes were made. Let me just say it was not my intent to do business with Khomeini, to trade weapons for hostages, nor to undercut our policy of antiterrorism.

Ronald Reagan, radio broadcast
(December 6, 1986)

Mistakes were made here by people who either did it deliberately or inadvertently. Now, others—it's up to others to decide whether those mistakes were made deliberately or inadvertently.

Bill Clinton, press conference (January 28, 1997)

Mistakes were made that cost my son's life and all I can say is I'm so sorry for what happened.

Brian Peterson, on trial with his girlfriend for
killing their infant son, in court testimony
(July 8, 1998)

If in hindsight we . . . discover that mistakes may have been made as regards prompt removal of priests and assistance to victims, I am deeply sorry.

Edward Cardinal Egan, archbishop of New
York, letter to parishioners on the Catholic
Church's pedophilia scandal (April 20–21, 2002)

In the night in the fog of war, mistakes were made.

General David Richards, commander, NATO
International, Security Assistance Force, state-
ment on accidental killing of Afghan civilians in
a NATO bombing (October 28, 2006)

Mistakes were made initially, but they were in no way due to any political or partisan rationale.

> *Internal Revenue Service statement on inappro-*
> *priate scrutiny of conservative political groups*
> *(May 10, 2013)*

The last week has certainly tested this Administration. Mistakes were clearly made. And as a result, we let down the people we are entrusted to serve.

> *NJ Governor Chris Christie,*
> *State of the State Address (January 10, 2014)*

At least the speakers of these grudging and expertly parsed admissions chose their words, in a narrow sense, skillfully. But students tend to use the passive voice merely as a bad habit, part of the pompous style. The usual result? Turgid prose:

Passive Voice	Active Voice
The Taft-Hartley Act was also used to support the Court's decision.	The Court also cited the Taft-Hartley Act.
While reading Mill's "On Liberty," the concept of personal freedom was discussed.	In "On Liberty," Mill discusses the concept of personal freedom.
The view of the mother is displayed when Garland writes, "She didn't want to leave our home and move west."	Garland says his mother "didn't want to leave our home and move west."
It was discussed in this reading that it is important for us to understand the people with whom we work.	Smith argues that it is important to understand the people we work with.
In the novel's early chapters, a large emphasis is placed upon his pride.	The novel's early chapters emphasize his pride.

Clarity and Honesty

The three techniques we've discussed for writing clearer prose work well most of the time and will help you develop a lively style. Violating them indiscriminately will saddle your readers with lifeless, shapeless sentences littered with prepositions and ugly, boring nouns (as nominalizations—even the name is ugly—usually are). Throw in big words, and you've got the full-blown pompous style.

Some people instinctively turn to the pompous style when things get rough. Consider an example from the Bible, when Moses returns to the Israelites after he has spent forty days on the mountaintop. He's bringing the Ten Commandments, but while he's been gone all hell has broken loose. The Israelites, feeling abandoned in the wilderness, have begun worshipping a new idol that Moses's brother, Aaron, made: a golden calf. Furious, Moses smashes the Ten Commandments and turns to Aaron, who was supposed to have been in charge during his absence. What happened?, he wants to know. Where did the golden calf come from? Aaron doesn't flat-out lie, but he tries to weasel out of his role in the debacle:

> And I said unto them, Whosoever hath any gold, let them break it off. So they gave it me: then I cast it into the fire, and there came out this calf. (Exod. 32:24)

There came out this calf. I've always wondered what look Moses gave Aaron after hearing this. (The Bible doesn't say.)

A twentieth-century example of using language the weasel way comes from Kosovo, 1999. A young Serbian man said this to an American reporter:

> We have to accept the facts. Very bad things happened in Kosovo, and we are going to pay for that. (Booth B5)

He starts off with a seemingly forthright acceptance of responsibility. Then comes a bit of weaseling with the no-agent agency of *very bad things happened*. But there's more: by rhetorically separating those *bad things* that happened from *we*—Serbians presumably—the sentence calls into question the legitimacy of holding that blurry *we* responsible. By the end of the statement the Serbs in Kosovo emerge not as victimizers but victims.

Human rights organizations tell us that in China (to take another example not on our doorstep), investigators routinely torture suspects during interrogation sessions. Chinese authorities don't like to admit this. Official transcripts of interrogation sessions in China thus require some reading between the lines:

Education takes place. (Rosenthal A10)

This bland, chilling statement could be Exhibit A in how to use words to conceal and evade.

No matter the technique for doing so, writing clearly is in the end not just a matter of technique or skill but of will. "The great enemy of clear language," Orwell said, "is insincerity" (1968, 137). Clarity is an ethical imperative. It takes honesty to say what we see and think, and courage to tell the truth. The ethics of clarity hold for college students no less than for diplomats, police, soldiers, politicians, and CEOs. How you choose to speak and write in school shapes how you will act—and what you will become—later in life.

3 Flow

AN ESSAY IS made of passages, and a passage, as its name implies, involves motion—movement from point A to point B. A reader is thus a kind of traveler. If the writer has done his job, the travel will prove worthwhile and maybe even entertaining. On rare occasions the traveler may even feel magically transported by the grace of what she's reading. This feeling comes from hard work on the writer's part, yet there are tricks for getting a reader from A to B (or Z for that matter), for achieving writing that seems to flow. Consider the following:

Original	Revision
Denial, anger, bargaining, depression, and acceptance are among the five stages of the process of grief, said a psychiatrist named Elisabeth Kübler-Ross in her book *On Death and Dying.* Many people were influenced by the book, which was published in 1969 and was a bestseller. A refusal to accept the outcome commences the process. . . .	In *On Death and Dying* (1969), the Swiss psychiatrist Elisabeth Kübler-Ross popularized the notion of grief as a process. According to Kübler-Ross there are five stages of grief: denial, anger, bargaining, depression, and acceptance. In the first stage, denial. . . .

The original's ungainly first sentence lists terms before offering any explanation or background. *Among* implies a partial list, and the reader may skip back and count the terms (we want the reader moving forward, not backward). Instead of building a bridge from the list to the last sentence by repeating the terms *denial* and *stage*, the original passage uses different words; its *refusal to accept* in place of *denial* is a distracting echo of a different term. The original's second sentence, on the book's influence, takes up too much space and diverts attention from the paragraph's main function, introducing Kübler-Ross's ideas.

The revision divides the long first sentence in two, shaping the flow of information and allowing a pause after introductory material. Its sentences end emphatically. The revision distills the original second sentence into one word, *popularized*. Its third sentence builds links by repeating important terms, *stage* and *denial*. All of this helps speed the reader on.

In this chapter we'll look at four techniques for achieving flow in your writing: (1) deploying consistent and logical characters, (2) using pronouns and other pointers, (3) designing sentences with punch lines, and (4) signaling logical steps in your argument with conjunctions and other linking words. These four techniques will help you write prose that is easier to read and understand.

Use Consistent Characters

Good essays unfold like stories—not in the sense of being dramatic or exciting, but in the sense of showing characters doing things or being described. Here is a passage about the American political system in the nineteenth century:

> The American system Bryce was describing was one whose regulations were few, whose resources were many, and whose central government was unobtrusive. It was a system ideally suited for congressional government. (Theodore Lowi, *The End of Liberalism*)

American system binds this passage together, not just because it is the subject of both sentences, but because of those little words like *one*, *whose*, and *it* that point back to it. Note too how the passage ends by handing off, as it were, to a new character: *congressional government*.

The lesson is that you need to control how your reader moves from one character to the next. The next example fails to do that. It presents a jumble of characters, bringing the reader's thinking to a halt as he struggles to figure out who is doing what:

Original

> Machiavelli's view of Christianity comes from a political standpoint. Morality is taken into little consideration when religion is discussed in his works.

Even though it sticks to a single topic, the passage feels choppy. The revision addresses the profusion of characters by building upon one, *Machiavelli*:

Revision

Machiavelli judges religion from a political standpoint. He virtually ignores the moral teachings of Christianity.

Here's another example of how thinking about characters can make a passage easier to read. We'll go through several revisions, to see how writing can improve step-by-step:

Original	Revision 1
The idea from Macgregor's book that stands out is the fact that there is self-control and self-direction.	Macgregor emphasizes self-control and self-direction.

The revision makes Macgregor the character—a much better choice than an abstract character like *idea* or *fact*. But more revision is called for. Since it isn't clear whose *self-control and self-direction* Macgregor means, the writer identifies another important character:

Revision 2

Macgregor emphasizes self-control and self-direction on the part of employees.

Better, but *self-control and self-direction on the part of employees* is ungainly, so the writer seeks a better term and considers making *employees* a more active character. This prompts further thinking, and the writer decides to provide more detail about what employees feel and why it matters:

Revision 3

Macgregor argues that employees who feel a sense of autonomy will have higher motivation and productivity.

Exploring a single topic often means treating several different characters. An essay about continental drift, for instance, needs to explain the process by considering the structures and dynamics of the earth's surface and interior. Its sequence of characters might look like this:

the earth's surface → parts of the surface (oceans and continents) →
continental drift → forces driving continental drift → the earth's mantle
→ the earth's crust → plates

We might encounter these characters in a passage like this:

> The earth looks unchanging, but it is not. The Atlantic Ocean, for in-
> stance, is spreading by about two centimeters a year. The continent of
> Africa is being slowly torn apart down its middle, at the Great Rift Valley.
> India is gradually crashing into Asia, a pileup that created and is still lifting
> the Himalayas. The whole surface of the earth is in flux, as the continents
> crash together and pull apart. This process, long dismissed as a fantasy
> but confirmed in recent decades, is called continental drift. Over hundreds
> of millions of years it has reshaped the surface of the earth.
>
> Continental drift is caused by the motion of convection currents in the
> earth's mantle, a layer of molten rock that lies beneath the crust. The crust
> itself is not solid, but consists of rigid slabs or plates. . . .

In the following passage from an economics paper, the student thought
she was sticking to one topic, the benefits of foreign trade, but the passage
lacks flow because it treats characters sloppily. It begins and ends with
one character, China, but switches in the middle to another, the United
States (denoted with an adjective and an unacademic *we*):

> China stands to gain from increasing trade. Throughout the 1990s, 30 per-
> cent of American economic growth came from foreign trade (Garten 23).
> With the opening of China's markets, we stand to have even more eco-
> nomic growth from overseas, while China will also benefit greatly.

Either character, China or the United States, may be the appropriate one
to focus on, depending on the writer's intentions—or both, perhaps, in
successive paragraphs or sections. The key is to select and move among
characters according to a sensible design.

Use Pronouns and Other Pointers

Inexperienced writers tend to prefer big words to little ones. But experienced writers, less anxious to show off their learning with every word,
make frequent use of some of the shortest and humblest words in

English—definite pronouns, possessive adjectives, relative pronouns, and relative adjectives. These little words point (or relate), in their respective ways, to something already named or known (an antecedent). The pointer might function as a subject of its clause (e.g., I, you, he, she, it, we, you, they, who, that, which, this, that) or as its object (e.g., me, you, him, her, it, us, you, them, whom, this, that). The pointer can refer to the antecedent in its own right or merely in its capacity as a possessor of something (e.g., my, your, his, her, its, our, your, their, whose). The beauty of these little words is that they eliminate the need to repeat the antecedent; they allow you to focus attention on the antecedent's qualities or actions:

> As Mahayana Buddhism spread across Asia, **it** came into contact with peoples of many different cultures and mentalities **who** interpreted the Buddha's doctrine from **their own** point of view, elaborating many of **its** subtle points in great detail and adding **their own** original ideas. In **this** way **they** kept Buddhism alive over the centuries and developed highly sophisticated philosophies with profound psychological insights. (Fritjof Capra, *The Tao of Physics*, emphasis added)

Humble pronouns and other pointers permit powerful effects. The historian William Manchester, for instance, concludes a dense and detailed paragraph on European power politics in the 1930s with a strong sentence built on a relative pronoun: "This was the final blow to appeasement." Inexperienced writers tend not to trust the power of such simple effects, even going out of their way to avoid them:

Original

Hamlet wrestles with his identity while trying to fulfill the ghost's demand for revenge. Hamlet loves to learn and asks questions about everything. But Hamlet's search for knowledge conflicts with his sense of filial duty.

Little words make the revision more flowing and more sophisticated:

Revision

Hamlet wrestles with his identity while trying to fulfill the ghost's demand for revenge. He loves to learn and asks questions about everything. But his search for knowledge conflicts with his sense of filial duty.

A pronoun must match its antecedent. Failing to do this is a common but easy-to-fix mistake. Here, the pronoun *they* doesn't match the antecedent:

> Machiavelli feels that Paganism favored freedom. They praised glory and war, unlike Christians. More inclined to fight fiercely, they were better able to defend freedom.

The writer assumed that referring to *Paganism* established the idea of *Pagans*, the implied antecedent for *they*. But this won't do. Though it isn't especially difficult, readers forced to make this little leap for themselves are likely to be a tad irritated. Revision is simple:

> Machiavelli feels that Paganism favored freedom. Pagans, unlike Christians, praised glory and war. More inclined to fight fiercely, they were better able to defend their freedom.

A complication arises: When must you repeat your noun, and when is it okay to continue to use pronouns? The answer is that you should return to the original noun any time an intervening noun may create confusion (*Christians* above wouldn't confuse anyone). In the original below, it's unclear to whom *he* refers, so the revision names the person:

Original	Revision
In Florence, Leonardo studied in the famed workshop of Andrea del Verrocchio. He had been trained as a goldsmith, and this proved to be a major influence on Leonardo's work.	In Florence, Leonardo studied in the famed workshop of Andrea del Verrocchio. Verrocchio had been trained as a goldsmith, and this proved to be a major influence on Leonardo's work.

As a stylistic matter, expect to use pronouns mostly *within* logical units, and to return to their antecedent nouns at natural emphasis points—the beginnings and ends of paragraphs, for instance.

Use Punch Lines

The same technique a comedian uses to make people laugh—careful setup and good punch line—can help you write sentences people like to read. Start with material that is familiar, scene-setting, or unsurprising, and end with material that is new or detailed or surprising (see also Williams 116–20). Here are two examples, one of which uses the punch-line technique to set up a joke, and the other to deliver a memorable phrase:

> In 1890, a railroad man from Cincinnati named Henry C. Bagley came to this part of Georgia, saw the stately white pines and poplars, and was so moved by their towering majesty and abundance that he decided to chop them all down. (Bill Bryson, *A Walk in the Woods*)

> In brief, the interpretive difficulties surrounding the Founder come to this: the image simultaneously embodies an almost sanctimonious piety and a murderous cruelty, both reverence and mayhem. (Hanna Fenichel Pitkin, *Fortune Is a Woman*)

Mind you, I'm not suggesting that every sentence should have this old-new structure, but it's a remarkably common pattern:

> Most physicists believe that matter is composed of particles called fermions.

> It has been said that the American Constitution is a system designed by geniuses to be run by idiots.

> What stands out in the account of Inca religion is the divine mission of the ruler.

The punch-line technique is even more useful in weaving separate sentences together. Let's look back at the example that opened this chapter:

Original	Revision
Denial, anger, bargaining, depression, and acceptance are among the five stages of the process of grief, said a psychiatrist named Elisabeth Kübler-Ross in her book *On Death and Dying*.	In *On Death and Dying* (1969), the Swiss psychiatrist Elisabeth Kübler-Ross popularized the notion of grief as a process. According to Kübler-Ross there are five stages of grief: denial, anger, bargaining, depression, and acceptance.

First the original reels off its list, and then it starts catching the reader up with the information needed to make sense of that list. The revision's two sentences, by contrast, start with scene-setting material and end with new ideas (*grief as a process* and *five stages of grief*). Note that even the arrangement of those two new ideas follows the same logic—first we learn about grief as a *process*, then we learn that this process consists of *five stages*.

When this punch-line technique is used to bind a paragraph, it's called a chain structure. Here's another example:

> Our bodies are composed of cells. The cells each have in them a nucleus. Within the nucleus are twenty-three pairs of chromosomes. In each pair, one chromosome came from the genetic mother and one from the genetic father. Located on the chromosomes are the genes, the basic units of heredity, composed of a kind of protein called DNA. Any particular gene of a parent may or may not be passed to a child. A gene passed on may or may not be "expressed"—that is, a child with the gene may or may not have the characteristic. A child can carry one parent's gene for blue eyes, and yet have brown eyes. (Barbara Katz Rothman, *Recreating Motherhood*)

This structure helps the reader absorb a lot of information without feeling overwhelmed.

Introductory Phrases

A related technique is to begin a sentence with an introductory prepositional phrase. Such phrases often date or place the main statement:

> By the middle of the sixth century BCE, the wave of colonial expansion was over.

> From the turn of the century to the 1960s, experimental psychologists treated the mind as a blank slate.

> In her youth Virginia Woolf chafed at the patriarchal boundaries of her father's world. [*Note that here the pronoun may precede the antecedent.*]

> In France the situation was much different.

> In these areas, people embraced Shang civilization but maintained political autonomy.

Or an introductory phrase may provide other kinds of contextual information:

> In this letter to his old friend, Jefferson seems tired and pessimistic. Behind the scenes there was confusion about how to respond.

> In practice, however, the president's power waxes and wanes with the election cycle

> According to Lacan, there is an active linguistic relationship between analyst and patient.

This last phrase, *according to x*, is an especially useful technique in academic writing, where one of the main challenges is synthesizing others' words and ideas without endorsing them as your own. In general, these opening phrases make room for contextual information, so that by the time you reach your main point your reader gets it. In writing, as in joke telling, timing matters.

Use Conjunctions and Other Linking Words

Introductory prepositional phrases lead naturally to our fourth and final technique for enhancing flow: conjunctions and other logical linking words. We'll consider two similar kinds of links, conjunctions and conjunctive adverbs. Conjunctions—everyday words like *and, but*, and *or*—show relations between words, phrases, or clauses. Conjunctive adverbs—dressy academic words like *furthermore, although, on the other hand*, and *in conclusion*—tend to take up more space and draw more attention to themselves. Both are part of an essay's metadiscourse—messages to the reader about what direction the argument is taking. They help prose feel connected from sentence to sentence. Writers who don't know how to use links well use only the simplest, like *also*: *Also, Touchstone tries to get out of marrying Audrey.* Or they repeat key terms from one sentence to the next, which is likely to give prose a plodding feel. Consider the following paper from a business class. Having just listed a company's strengths, the writer now turns to its weaknesses:

Original	Revision
Also, Disney has its share of weaknesses. One of Disney's potential weaknesses is the idea that the company may be facing the need for a new CEO in the next couple of years.	Despite these strengths, Disney does have its share of weaknesses. First, the company may soon need a new CEO.

Also is a poor choice, since it doesn't fit the logical turn the essay is taking (the revision's *Despite* is much more helpful). The original links its two sentences by repeating a key word, *weaknesses*. By contrast, the revision uses a conjunctive adverb, *First*, and trusts the reader to remember the topic (note as well the other changes that make the revision more concise and active).

Inexperienced writers tend to overuse vague links:

Earlier it was mentioned that . . . as commented on earlier . . . as stated earlier . . . as stated before . . . as I wrote before . . .

In a short essay these retrospective phrases are about as useful as stapling one sheet of paper. (If you feel you really need such a link—say, in a longish term paper—better choices might be *as noted above*, *as we've seen*, or *as we've suggested*.)

Now let's look at more effective ways of linking with conjunctions and conjunctive adverbs. In practice we're not much interested in the distinction between these types of links, except insofar as you know how to use and punctuate each term.[1] It's more important to have a sense of the kinds of turns an argument can take, and the links that may be used to signal them. Here is a reasonably complete list of logical turns and links.

---

1. Grammatically, conjunctions can bear some of the weight of joining clauses together, and often work with commas. But conjunctive adverbs require a full stop (like a period or semicolon) between clauses. A common mistake is to treat conjunctive adverbs like conjunctions and attach them with a comma: *The findings weren't conclusive, however they do suggest that the document was altered.* This needs a semicolon before *however* (and a comma afterward, most authorities would advise).

1. **Continuity** or **amplification** *(also, and, besides, furthermore, in addition, in the same way, likewise, moreover, not only . . . but also, similarly, too)*

> Recent British novels, too, have been interested in the history of the creatures as part of our natural history. (A. S. Byatt, *On Histories and Stories*)

> The king, moreover, had little reason to call Parliament into session as long as he could raise funds through other means.

2. **Contrast** *(against, although, but, by contrast, conversely, despite, however, in contrast, instead, nevertheless, nonetheless, on the contrary, on the other hand, otherwise, still, though, yet)*

> But if in some ways Arendt stands with the Frankfurt School's critique of modernity, she is simultaneously in the other camp as well. . . . (Margaret Canovan, *Hannah Arendt*)

> Despite these setbacks, Mao's power grew steadily.

> Pagan beliefs and practices nevertheless persisted in rural areas. The findings were not conclusive; they do suggest, however, that the document was altered.

> Nonspecialists will have trouble with this text, however.

3. **Conditionality** *(if)*

> If one imagines oneself in Claudius's position, one realizes that he is just as much a prisoner of Elsinore as Hamlet is.

4. **Time** and **frequency** *(after, afterward, at the same time, before, during this time, earlier, eventually, later, meanwhile, now, subsequently, then, at times, frequently, often, once, once again, sometimes, rarely)*

> The duke's position was now untenable.

5. **Logical order** *(finally, first, first of all, last, last of all, less obviously, more importantly, primarily, second, second of all)*

> First of all, we should ask why the individual needs a cognitive map of his or her city.

6. **Example** *(for example, for instance, in particular)*

> Ben Jonson, for instance, extensively revised his manuscripts before publication.

7. **Reality check** *(actually, apparently, indeed, in fact, ostensibly, supposedly, to be sure)*

> In fact there is little evidence to support her interpretation. Ostensibly, they never discussed the lawsuit during these meetings.

8. **Cause** *(as, because, for, for this reason, since)*

> Since none of Pythagoras's writings have survived, we only know of him at second hand.

9. **Consequence** *(accordingly, as a result, as this suggests, by this means, consequently, hence, here, in this manner, so, then, thereby, therefore, thus)*

> None of Pythagoras's writings have survived. Consequently, we only know of him at second hand.

> Cultural awareness, thus, is a vital management skill.

10. **Conclusion** *(all in all, and so, as a general rule, finally, generally, in brief, in conclusion, in fine, in other words, in short, in sum, in the end, so, then, to conclude, to sum up)*

> In sum, there seems to be a long-standing consensus in the United States that job discrimination is wrong.

> Clinton's presidency, in short, had been critically weakened.

As you can see, there are many ways to deploy links—too many to let us boil the technique down to a few rules. Beyond these examples, the best way to learn is to read and read and read: see how good writers create flowing prose.

4 Punctuation

PUNCTUATION IS THE use of signs to help readers understand and express written matter. It includes things like capital letters, commas, indented first lines of paragraphs, and spaces between words—all the routine devices that help readers decipher prose quickly and accurately. Because the idea of punctuation arose long after the invention of writing itself, ancient texts lack most of the aids to comprehension that we take for granted:

IMAGINEREADINGTHISWITHNOCLUESABOUTWHERETOPAU
SEORWHEREANEWTOPICSTARTSORWHEREONESENTEN
CEENDSANDANOTHERBEGINS

Modern American punctuation is a kind of living history of Western culture. It is composed of practices and innovations developed by ancient writers, medieval monks, Norman conquerors, Renaissance humanists, Enlightenment rationalists, American grammarians, and ordinary speakers of American English. Over time new marks and devices have appeared and changed, and standards of punctuation have changed as well. An eighteenth-century version of this text, for instance, would seem to us to have far too many commas. Indeed the rules of punctuation, which many people mistake for timeless expressions of pure logic, are better understood as the product of an ongoing tug-of-war between reason, custom, and fickle fashion.

But for students and scholars, appealing to history does little good. Defying today's punctuation rules is perceived by readers as a sign of ignorance or carelessness, two cardinal sins in the academic world. Thus it's prudent to treat the rules of punctuation as if they really were commandments graven in stone. This chapter will consider the essentials of punctuation: the rules and customs governing commas and comma splices, semicolons, colons, dashes, parentheses, and question marks. (We'll deal with the complexities of quotation marks, as well as ellipses and brackets, in Chapter 6.)

But punctuation is more than an arbitrary system of rules. Its purpose is to help your reader make sense of what you've written. Within the rules there are more and less effective ways to use punctuation to guide your reader through your prose. Consider this example. Both the original and the revision obey the rules of punctuation. But the original, relying solely on periods, is less clear than the revision, which employs several techniques to order the same material:

Original	Revision
In the thirteenth century governments joined in the repression of the Jews. The Fourth Lateran Council required Jews to wear distinctive dress. Jewish books were burned. Official expulsions began. The Jews were banished from England in 1290. They were not to return until the seventeenth century.	In the thirteenth century, governments joined in the repression of the Jews: the Fourth Lateran Council required Jews to wear distinctive dress, Jewish books were burned, and official expulsions began— Jews were banished from England in 1290 and were not to return until the seventeenth century.

While both of these passages are correct, the revision provides punctuation clues about how to arrange and connect its facts.

Commas and Comma Splices

Commas allow one to create long, complex sentences that are still readable:

> In an astonishing late-fifteenth-century panel by Hieronymus Bosch, now in the Doge's Palace in Venice, we see naked souls that have been cleansed of their sins lifted by angels toward a long funnel, a kind of birth canal, at whose end figures are emerging into a blinding light. (Stephen Greenblatt, *Hamlet in Purgatory*)

The commas create pauses that allow the reader to follow the dense description without too much strain.

Commas are so flexible that rules for using them are complicated. Some of the rules are easy: use commas to separate items in a list, for instance. But should you put a comma before the list's last item? *Landis, Kuhn, and Selig* or *Landis, Kuhn and Selig*? Some authorities insist on such terminal commas; others avoid them. It's safest to be conservative and use terminal commas until you know what's expected of you in a given situation.

We can break comma rules into four categories—when not to use them, when you may use them, when you should use them, and when you must use them.

No Comma Allowed

Don't put commas between subject and verb, adjective and noun, verb and direct object, or between any such close pair of grammatical elements. Not this: *The mosque, was built in 1547.*

Exception: A *pair* of commas can be used to insert words even between closely linked grammatical elements. The idea is that the pair of commas works rather like parentheses to mark beginning and end, so even a lengthy intrusion shouldn't lead the reader astray: *The mosque, located on the site of a pagan temple that according to archeological evidence dated back perhaps as far as the third millennium BCE, was built in 1547.*

You may not use a comma by itself to punctuate between two complete statements; this is the dreaded comma splice:

Comma Splice

Deception runs through *Measure for Measure*, the duke sets the tone by pretending to be a priest.

There are many ways to fix comma splices. Here are some:

Deception runs through *Measure for Measure*. The duke sets the tone by pretending to be a priest.

Deception runs through *Measure for Measure*; the duke sets the tone by pretending to be a priest.

Deception runs through *Measure for Measure*, and the duke sets the tone by pretending to be a priest.

Some authorities permit comma splices to join short sentences, but it is prudent for anyone writing for an American academic audience to avoid them altogether.

The final prohibition on commas concerns *restrictive* modifiers—words, phrases, and clauses that *restrict* or specify the meaning of a noun, and are thus essential to the sentence's meaning. Restrictive modifiers may not be set off with commas:

Wrong	Right
Employees, vested in the pension plan, had more control over their money than is generally realized.	Employees vested in the pension plan had more control over their money than is generally realized.

Since the phrase specifies *which* employees, it restricts or is essential to understanding, and so does not take commas. (The underlying idea, of course, is that a pair of commas indicates that what they set off provides supplementary, not vital, information.)

Comma Optional

Commas are used in tandem with coordinating conjunctions (*and, but, for,* and so on) to connect independent clauses:

> In the seventh century trade across the Channel and the North Sea was beginning to be important, and there are signs that it was becoming organized.

But you may sometimes prefer to skip the comma and keep the sentence moving. This happens often with *and*:

> In 1254 the last Hohenstaufen, Conrad IV, was killed and an interregnum began in the Holy Roman Empire which was to last until the election of Count Rudolf of Habsburg as king of the Romans in 1273.

The writer decided that the nearness of the appositive's commas to the conjunction made another pause unnecessary. Cut the appositive, and one would be more likely to put a comma at the conjunction:

> In 1254 Conrad IV was killed, and an interregnum began in the Holy Roman Empire which was to last until the election of Count Rudolf of Habsburg as king of the Romans in 1273.

In general, think of commas as places where your reader can catch her breath. After certain introductory phrases and at other places, a sentence may or may not benefit from such a pause. The commas in these sentences, for instance, are matters of judgment:

> Not surprisingly, the deception was soon discovered.

> First of all, let us consider the evidence in favor of this interpretation. He left Russia in 1918, and spent several years in Europe and America. The lesson is, or should be, clear. [Either both commas or none.]

Comma Preferred

Lengthy introductory phrases are easier to absorb if followed by a comma:

> Despite his protestations that he had done nothing wrong, the comptroller was fired.

Comma Mandatory

Appositives must generally be enclosed with commas:

> One man, Gandhi, resolved to change this.

> Plautus, perhaps the most important of the Roman playwrights, had an immense influence on Western literature and drama.

(For more on appositives, see the next chapter.)

Nonrestrictive modifiers—that is, words, phrases, and clauses that provide supplementary information rather than serve an essential informational purpose—must be set off by commas:

> The document, which has never been scientifically analyzed or dated, is kept in an old vault in the monastery.

Rembrandt, whose fortunes fluctuated wildly over the years, declared himself bankrupt in 1656.

The difference between restrictive and nonrestrictive modifiers boils down to whether the modifying phrase is central to the sentence's meaning:

Restrictive	Nonrestrictive
Congressmen who take money from illicit sources must be identified and punished.	Congressmen, who take money from all sorts of donors, must be held to high standards.
The modifier narrows the scope of the noun, by specifying a subset of Congressmen. Thus the modifier is **restrictive** *and essential: do not use commas.*	*The modifier does not narrow the scope of the noun, for it refers to all Congressmen. Thus the modifier is* **nonrestrictive** *and supplementary: use commas.*

You should also use commas when you reverse customary arrangements of information, for instance putting a country before a city:

Owen was born in England, in a small town called Oswestry.

Had you followed "normal" order, you would not need a comma:

Owen was born in the small town of Oswestry in England.

Finally, to avoid confusion it's important to keep modifiers close to what they modify:

Wrong	Right
Schwartz argued that in the modern world the poet, writing on the eve of the Second World War, must look within for inspiration.	Schwartz, writing on the eve of the Second World War, argued that in the modern world the poet must look within for inspiration.
	Writing on the eve of the Second World War, Schwartz argued that in the modern world the poet must look within for inspiration.

Semicolons

Like a period, a semicolon signals the end of an independent clause—
but it also indicates a link of some kind to the next clause:

> Fears of an impending catastrophe, Lomborg argues, are wildly exagger-
> ated. Agricultural production per head has risen; the numbers facing
> starvation have declined.

> In his poetry Frost crafted an image of himself as a self-reliant New
> England farmer, chopping wood and patching fences; but in truth his
> grandfather helped pay for his studies, travels, and writing.

> In 1983 President Reagan upset respectable opinion by calling the Soviet
> Union an "evil empire"; just a few years later, when it abruptly collapsed,
> his words seemed not reactionary but prescient.

Used well, a semicolon suggests that the writer is building an argument,
not just piling on sentences. Lewis Thomas, a gifted essayist, nicely
expresses the semicolon's appeal:

> It is almost always a greater pleasure to come across a semicolon than a
> period. The period tells you that that is that; if you didn't get all the mean-
> ing you wanted or expected, anyway you got all the writer intended to
> parcel out and now you have to move along. But with a semicolon there
> you get a pleasant little feeling of expectancy; there is more to come; read
> on; it will get clearer. (Lewis Thomas, "Notes on Punctuation")

In the following passage Thomas (a physician who wrote essays about
science and biology) uses a series of semicolons to punctuate his description of the body's internal workings.

> Secretory cells elaborate their products in privacy; the heart contracts and
> relaxes; hormones are sent off to react silently with cell membranes,
> switching adenyl cyclase, prostaglandin, and other signals on and off;
> cells communicate with each other by simply touching; organelles send
> messages to other organelles; all this goes on continually, without ever a
> personal word from us. The arrangement is that of an ecosystem, with the
> operation of each part being governed by the state and function of all the
> other parts. (Lewis Thomas, *The Lives of a Cell*)

The series of semicolons—full stops that are also links—subtly reinforces Thomas's argument about the systemic interaction of the body's organs, which he wishes to portray as both autonomous and interdependent. As we've observed, we tend to interpret writing as having good style when its grammar suits its message.

Finally, semicolons also replace commas in a list when one or more of the items has an internal comma:

Wrong	Right
Leviathan has many unforgettable passages: Hobbes's evocation of a savage state of nature, his establishment of a binding, permanent social contract to protect individuals, and his refusal to limit the power of the ruler.	*Leviathan* has many unforgettable passages: Hobbes's evocation of a savage state of nature; his establishment of a binding, permanent social contract to protect individuals; and his refusal to limit the power of the ruler.

Colons

Most frequently used as terminal punctuation (that is, to mark the end of an independent clause), colons announce an immediate logical link between statements. Often the clause preceding the colon implicitly asks a question that is answered by what follows, which may or may not be a complete statement:

> Machiavelli thus faces a dilemma: the lust for power builds states but also threatens to destroy them.

> The secret of Wal-Mart's success is simple: state-of-the-art inventory management.

> Rat fleas are greatly affected by temperature and humidity: their numbers dwindle in hot, dry summers and increase in cooler, more humid months.

> But places have meanings: They are seen and interpreted through a social-cultural filter. (Edward Krupat, *People in Cities*)

Colons are sometimes used for rhetorical effect, and in these cases usage permits more flexibility about what falls on either side of the colon:

To repeat: there is no alternative.

As you know, under our three-branch system of government, the tax laws are created by: Satan. (Dave Barry)

Colons also introduce lists. To do this right you need an independent clause (a statement that can stand on its own) preceding the colon:

Wrong	Right
The problems were:	There were two problems:
Several economic agreements are especially significant, such as:	Several economic agreements are especially significant:

Finally, colons are often used to introduce quotations. As with lists, the statement preceding the colon must be able to stand by itself. In modern American usage the common "x says" construction to introduce a quotation takes a comma, not a colon:

Wrong	Right
Queen Elizabeth says:	Queen Elizabeth says, / Queen Elizabeth addresses her army:
She explained:	She explained, / She explained it as follows:

For more on quotations, see Chapter 6.

Dashes

Dashes differ from hyphens, which are a these-words-go-together device for stapling together compound adjectives. Dashes separate words—they force the reader to pause right where the writer wants him to. Flexible and flashy, dashes are a favorite of many writers. They can replace any of the punctuation marks we've looked at:

That is the critical point—what the test measures is not absolute intelligence but cultural literacy.

The texts students read, the kind of thinking necessary to work through complex arguments, and what students must do to show adequate mastery of the material—all lead naturally to an emphasis on critical thinking and writing skills.

During Machiavelli's lifetime, Italy as a single political entity did not exist—instead, there was a patchwork of city-states, petty kingdoms, republics, duchies, and ecclesiastical states, constantly at war with one another.

Dashes often come in pairs, letting the writer return to the main flow as quickly as she left it. As with pairs of commas, make sure to return precisely to where you left the main grammatical structure:

In the era of globalization a disturbance in one country's economy can hurt—or destroy—a company on the other side of the globe.

There is a type of creative mind that finds sheer faithful copying—the translator's virtue—harder than fresh creation, and I consider that Shakespeare had this type of mind. (Anthony Burgess, *Shakespeare*)

Nineteenth-century American writers—Hawthorne, Melville, Emerson, and Poe chief among them—saw themselves as pioneers discovering or inventing a new kind of literature.

With the rise of outsourcing and the gig economy, loyalty to corporations—and their loyalty to employees—seems to be at an all-time low.

Machiavelli, obsessed with warfare—an obsession that one finds in all his writings, even his poems and plays—reflected the stark realities of power in Renaissance Italy.

Parentheses

Parentheses are like a pause button. The first parenthesis pauses the flow of your sentence, letting you insert tangential or supplementary material. Then, the second parenthesis signals a return to the sentence in midstream:

In the past Iraq produced a whole range of potent biological agents and toxins including anthrax (using strains originally ordered from American germ banks) and botulinum toxin.

Rather than duplicating services that established institutions were already providing (and might provide better), Spence focused on customer service management, and formed alliances between her company and a range of other care providers.

Parentheses also serve to enclose references:

Ruhe has constructed a two-dimensional model of this efficiency-effectiveness dynamic (Figure 1).

Make sure that you put spaces outside parentheses: not(this), but (this). A punctuation mark usually follows parentheses (without a space).

When the parenthetical element stretches for a sentence or more, it is typically set apart after the preceding sentence's punctuation:

Abu Bakr and Umar would hardly have recognized the Caliphate in its Baghdad incarnation, the wine-women-magic-carpet world of *The Thousand and One Nights*. (Neither, for that matter, would today's visitor to the sprawling, dusty, and largely charmless contemporary capital of Iraq recognize it as a once-splendid capital of a great empire.) (Thomas Lippman, *Understanding Islam*)

Parentheticals should be used sparingly in academic writing.

Questions

Inexperienced writers often think that direct questions are too lively for formal academic writing, and that they may only employ indirect questions, like this: *Throughout this book we have asked why some people love the city while others hate it.* Indirect questions have their uses, but direct questions are also legitimate and can be remarkably effective in formal writing. They precisely direct the reader's attention:

The Korean War prompted the civil and military leaders of the West to ask themselves some basic questions: What sort of war, or rather what sorts of wars, should we now prepare for? What are the ends and the means of our strategy? (Raymond Aron, *On War*)

How does language affect the brain? In *Language, Thought and Reality*, Benjamin Lee Whorf claimed that the structure of a language determines the reality we perceive. . . . (Robert Ornstein, *The Right Mind*)

A sequence of indirect question followed by direct question can be useful for emphasis:

Thus, the question arises why Locke and all his successors, their own insights notwithstanding, clung so obstinately to labor as the origin of property, of wealth, of all values and, finally, of the very humanity of man. Or, to put it another way, what were the experiences inherent in the laboring activity that proved of such great importance to the modern age? (Hannah Arendt, *The Human Condition*)

In the next example, the writer uses a different sort of two-question sequence: first a short, punchy question, and then a longer, more detailed version of essentially the same question. The result is an elegant sequence that leaves the reader with a clear idea of where the essay is going:

Rather than concern ourselves with the specifics of Columbia's design (see Altman & Cherners, 1980 . . .), we will pose the bottom-line question: Does it work? To what extent does systematic and comprehensive planning resolve or eliminate the problems of urban and suburban living? Not surprisingly, the answer is mixed. . . . (Edward Krupat, *People in Cities*)

Finally, questions can also serve a summative function, helping the reader digest what you've just argued even as you point the way ahead:

How will all this change the company and the economy as we know it? Jerusalem was now in Christian hands; but what was to become of the crusaders?

Well, if burial is no proof of symbolic activity, what else might we look for? (Ian Tattersall, *Becoming Human*)

Because they are so effective at focusing attention and announcing a new topic, questions are a common device at the beginnings of paragraphs.

5 Gracefulness

ONE OF THE great paradoxes of writing is that content is inseparable from style, even if we might formally distinguish the two. There is no such thing as "pure" content, as qualitatively neutral as a string of numbers. *What* we say, in other words, is intimately tied to *how* we say it. "A crowd has a generalized stink," said the poet W. H. Auden. "The public is odorless." At every turn, a writer faces a dizzying array of choices about which words to use and how to use them. We may seem to be setting out on firm ground, armed with a definite message and hard-and-fast rules of grammar and syntax, yet we soon find ourselves relying at least as much on our own feel for how best to put that message to any given audience.

Words matter. That is why every good writer should have some understanding of how to write gracefully—and how to use rhetoric to do so. In common parlance, *rhetoric* means bombastic, exaggerated, or empty language. But for those who think about writing and communication, it means something more specific: the science or art of persuasion by means of stylistic or structural techniques. Rhetoric has a long and checkered history. In his satire *Clouds*, the ancient Greek playwright Aristophanes associated rhetoric with making the weaker argument appear the stronger—an association it carries to this day. But rhetoric has also had its champions, like the ancient Roman statesman Cicero, for example, a great practitioner and theoretician of the art. Like it or not, all writers use rhetoric; given the nature of language, they have no alternative.

Even simplicity, which appears consciously nonrhetorical, is itself a rhetorical choice. In English literature, simplicity is most often associated with the so-called plain style, a style perfected in the seventeenth century and deployed in opposition to fancier—and by implication decadent—styles. George Orwell, a master of the twentieth-century plain style, adapted this style to brilliant effect in his political journalism and novels like *1984* and *Animal Farm*. Orwell's bare-bones plainness gives his writing an immediacy and authenticity perfectly suited to his master theme of individual against the system. The contemporary plain style I've been advocating is no less rhetorical and no less suited to writing effectively and gracefully in the twenty-first century. This chapter presents several techniques for making academic prose plainer and more graceful: (1) the historical present, (2) appositives, (3) parallelism, (4) tricolon, (5) concession, and (6) qualification (if you want to study rhetoric more thoroughly, see Corbett and Connors).

The Historical Present

Should you discuss a text in the present or past tense? At first blush it seems natural to frame the discussion in the past tense, but most textual analysis and commentary is written in a form of the present tense called the historical present (or literary present):

> Plato asks why one would choose to be good if there were no risk in being wicked.

> Hamlet tells Ophelia he never loved her.

> Donne frequently challenges his reader's expectations about textual integrity.

> Southey undermines the meaning of this "famous victory," so that by the end of the poem the children seem wiser than the man, who just echoes conventional opinion. Not the battle but the children's unanswered question—"But what good came of it at last?"—is what the poem wants us to remember.

And just to complicate matters, the historical present isn't the only tense used to discuss a work. When presenting facts about its composition—particularly if these include a date or time reference—use the past tense. In both of the following examples the author's action is tied to a specific time, and thus the past tense is appropriate:

Original	Revision
Machiavelli writes *The Prince* in 1513.	Machiavelli wrote *The Prince* in 1513.
Efforts to define and protect individual liberty have a long history. A century before the American Constitution, the English philosopher John Locke articulates a vision of liberal government in his *Second Treatise of Government.*	Efforts to define and protect individual liberty have a long history. A century before the American Constitution, the English philosopher John Locke articulated a vision of liberal government in his *Second Treatise of Government.*

Let's continue with that second example. If you went on to discuss Locke's *Second Treatise*, you would probably wish to switch to the historical present after the initial mention:

> Efforts to safeguard individual liberty have a long history. A century before the American Constitution was written, the English philosopher John Locke articulated a vision of liberal government in his *Second Treatise of Government.* In this famous work, Locke locates the origins of government in the desire to protect individuals and their property from the violence and insecurity of the state of nature. . . .

Clearly, judgment is called for. The longer you discuss a text, the likelier you should do so in the historical present. The briefer the discussion (suppose for instance that in the passage above, you finished with Locke and now turned to another work), the likelier the past tense will strike the reader as appropriate.

Appositives

It's often useful to condense two independent clauses into one. When the two clauses share a common noun and one of the clauses merely identifies that noun, you can gracefully condense the two clauses by way of an appositive. An appositive is a noun phrase used to identify another noun; it lets you insert an identifying clause stripped of any linking verb into a sentence built upon a more interesting verb. Devoting an entire sentence to identifying a person or concept, after all, takes up space. And, as we've seen, sentences built upon linking verbs often make for dull prose no matter how interesting their content. Appositives help make your writing tighter and more interesting.

Original	Revision
Huygens was one of the most remarkable Dutch personages of the seventeenth century. Huygens visited the young Rembrandt in 1626.	Huygens, one of the most remarkable Dutch personages of the seventeenth century, visited the young Rembrandt in 1626.
Slavery was already a vital part of the economy and culture of the Republic. It cannot be blamed for the subsequent decline of the Roman Empire.	Slavery, already a vital part of the economy of the Republic, cannot be blamed for the subsequent decline of the Roman Empire.
Right-hemisphere damage can leave the individual lacking a key part of what makes us human. This is the ability to understand others' feelings.	Right-hemisphere damage can leave the individual lacking a key part of what makes us human—the ability to understand others' feelings.

In the third instance, note that the appositive links back not simply to the word *human*, but to the whole phrase, *a key part. . . .*

Appositives can be linked together:

Angelou's novel ends with a return to Ghana, a powerful symbol for African Americans—the first African nation to throw off British colonial power.

An appositive can also serve to narrow or refine your focus:

But when low-status employees, especially women, file grievances, the results are quite different.

Appositives serve to identify sources elegantly and economically:

Original	Revision
George Gamow was a noted physicist and cosmologist. He was one of the early proponents of the big-bang theory. He argued that. . . .	George Gamow, the noted physicist and cosmologist, was one of the early proponents of the big-bang theory. He argued that. . . .
Matt Drudge is a controversial internet journalist. He says these concerns are groundless.	According to Matt Drudge, the controversial internet journalist, these concerns are groundless.

When an appositive supplies information that is not essential to the meaning of the sentence, it must be set off by either commas or dashes. (Use dashes if the appositive consists of a list of three or more items.) None of the appositives discussed so far in this section is essential to meaning; thus, all are set off by punctuation.

If an appositive *is* essential to meaning, it should not be set off by punctuation:

Original	Revision
President Kennedy had a brother named Robert. Robert served as attorney general.	President Kennedy's brother Robert served as attorney general.

The appositive *Robert* is essential because it identifies which brother served as attorney general. Had the president had only one brother, you would put commas around *Robert*.

Parallelism

One of the most flexible and useful of rhetorical devices, parallelism refers to the organizing of similar grammatical elements within some larger verbal structure so as to highlight the similarity of those elements. Such similarity can relate to any number of grammatical features. These might include number (singular or plural); parts of speech (noun, verb, adjective, adverb, preposition, interjection, conjunction); tense (e.g., present or past); mood (e.g., indicative or subjunctive); voice (active or passive); person (e.g., first or third), and so forth. Achieving parallelism in a sentence or paragraph requires consciously crafting key words, phrases, or entire clauses in such a way that they may be organized in parallel fashion. You might think of parallelism as involving a kind of rhetorical algebra; as the setting up of a proportion or the combining of like terms in an algebraic expression makes an equation easier to solve, parallelism makes a sentence easier to understand. Parallelism makes writing more comprehensible, graceful, and memorable.

> The prince's strength is also his weakness; his self-reliance is also isolation.

> In Machiavelli's world, Sheldon Wolin observes, moral ends have been replaced by ironies; answers have been replaced by questions.

> The characters are all watching one another, forming theories about one another, listening, contriving. . . .

> One side sees Lincoln as a bold and shrewd leader, sincerely committed to abolishing slavery; the other sees him as an opportunistic politician, concerned only to defend the union in any way possible.

> We take little note of the thousands of people who are polite, pleasant, or at least predictable; but we remember and accentuate our encounters with those who are rude, disagreeable, or strange. (Edward Krupat, *People in Cities*)

> We may finally define jurisprudence as the shining but unfulfilled dream of a world governed by reason. For some it lies buried in a system, the details of which they do not know. For some, familiar with the details of the system, it lies in the depth of an unread literature. For others, familiar with this literature, it lies in the hope of a future enlightenment. For all, it lies just around the corner. (Thurman Arnold, *The Symbols of Government*)

Faulty parallelism is a common problem, due mainly to carelessness. In the following examples the parallel elements in the revisions are italicized to make them easy to see:

Original	Revision
Someone acquiring knowledge is similar to finding a new path in a dense forest.	*Acquiring* knowledge is similar to *finding* a new path in a dense forest.
Machiavelli advocates relying on one's own strength, leaving as little to chance as possible, and the need to get rid of sentimental attachments.	Machiavelli advocates *relying* on one's own strength, *leaving* as little to chance as possible, and *ridding* oneself of sentimental attachments.
Touchstone satirizes courtly manners, woos Audrey, and he tries to avoid marriage.	Touchstone *satirizes* courtly manners, *woos* Audrey, and *tries to avoid* marriage.

Another common problem, this one stylistic rather than grammatical, is repeating too much in the parallel elements:

Original	Revision
Socrates led a private life, as opposed to a public life.	Socrates led a private rather than a public life.

When you arrange parallel elements, you can elegantly delete repeated words, leaving only the words that do not repeat. In the following examples, those words the respective writers left out have been struck through:

> Augustus wished to deceive the people by an image of civil liberty, and ~~he wished to deceive~~ the armies by an image of civil government. (Edward Gibbon, *The Decline and Fall of the Roman Empire*)

> Elephant shrews achieve sexual maturity in about five weeks, tenrecs ~~achieve sexual maturity~~ in two months.

Parallelism can be employed in many different ways. One technique is *chiasmus*, or inversion of parallel elements. A famous example comes from President John F. Kennedy's 1961 inaugural address:

> Ask not what your country can do for you—ask what you can do for your country.

College essays, of course, often develop arguments by presenting contrasting views. In such cases, parallelism offers a natural strategy for organizing the flow of words. In the following example, the writer identifies a particular debate, then uses parallel sentences to present each side in the debate:

> This rally sparked a fierce debate on Wall Street about whether a speculative bubble was emerging, and not just in Internet stocks but in the market at large. On one side were the traditionalists, who believed that stock prices had already risen well beyond levels that could be justified on the economic fundamentals. On the other side were the New Economy enthusiasts, who argued that the time-honored methods of valuing stocks no longer worked and should be discarded. (John Cassidy, "Striking It Rich")

Repetition of a word is a related technique. Here different forms of a word are used to create a sense of reflexivity:

> Tragedy explores the damage a damaged mind can do. (Ruth Padel, *Whom Gods Destroy*)

Tricolon

Tricolon is a particular kind of parallelism. The idea is simple: lists tend to feel balanced and complete when they contain three items. (People who think about how we process information, both visual and verbal, have long realized that three is a powerful and resonant number for pattern recognition.) Of course that doesn't mean you should wrench your material out of its natural arrangement to make it fit a tripartite scheme. Sometimes you'll want two, four, or more items in a list. But when you have flexibility in what to say, tricolon is often effective at making a list feel complete:

> Tribal or local heroes, such as the emperor Huang Ti, Moses, or the Aztec Tezcatlipoca, commit their boons to a single folk; universal heroes— Mohammed, Jesus, Gautama Buddha—bring a message for the entire world. (Joseph Campbell, *The Hero with a Thousand Faces*)

> A generation ago most scholars believed that an overarching worldview— conservative, deeply Christian, and essentially medieval in its commitment

to order and hierarchy—shaped the concerns and defined the intellectual limits of Shakespeare and other Elizabethan dramatists.

These two examples contain lists of nouns and adjectives, but tricolon may also be used for arranging other elements, like clauses:

> Coriolanus doesn't hide his contempt for the commoners; he doesn't flatter them; he doesn't try to soften his image.

Or sentences:

> Like the fool of Shakespearian drama, she fawns and flatters, reserving to herself the right to speak difficult truths that her demeanor and role appear to belie. Like the trickster of Afro-American folk culture, she speaks with a double tongue. Like the exile, she re-creates her own previous life as a function of her nostalgia. (Elizabeth Fox-Genovese, "My Statue, Myself: Autobiographical Writings of Afro-American Women")

Concession

Arguments are rarely airtight. Most admit of objections—based on, for example, the inconclusive nature of evidence cited (and thus the possibility of alternative interpretations) or the existence of contravening evidence. Inexperienced writers tend to sweep such inconveniences under the rug out of fear that calling attention to them might weaken their argument. But such a selective approach to representing evidence isn't always wise—especially if objections to an argument are obvious or well-known. Sometimes by conceding the limitations of one's argument, a writer actually strengthens it:

> Admittedly, there is no direct evidence that Shakespeare read Machiavelli.

The writer would present the objection in sufficient detail to fit the essay's depth of analysis. Then the writer would counter the objection, for instance along these lines:

But we know that many of Shakespeare's fellow playwrights did, that Shakespeare read at least some Italian, and that many of Machiavelli's works were easily available in London.

More purely rhetorical concessions, which have less to do with content and more with style and form, are also useful. Here the writer uses a concession as an elegant starting point for an essay:

> It may at first seem paradoxical to suggest that a company can increase its profits by putting moral values above financial results. How can it not hurt revenues to give workers more family leave and increase spending on employee benefits?

Here a writer criticizes American-led NATO bombing of Yugoslavia in 1999 for causing massive environmental harm. A predictable objection to her argument would be that Yugoslavia's environment had been damaged long before the bombing, due to decades of careless industrialization. In fact that objection is largely true, and she confronts it head on:

> In fairness, every international team doing environmental assessments in Yugoslavia has had difficulty distinguishing preexisting damage to soil and water systems from new toxins linked to the war. Long before the bombing, the Danube's viability was under siege from both industrial polluters to the north and 50 years of lax environmental oversight in Yugoslavia and the former Eastern Bloc nations. Scientists taking core sediment samples after the war have found toxins dating from the '60s, '70s and '80s—including contaminants related to the 1986 Chernobyl nuclear accident. But the NATO bombing unquestionably made the situation worse. Preexisting pollution is no reason to dismiss the environmental fallout from the war; it only makes the case for a cleanup more urgent. (Mitric B4)

Many less skilled writers would simply have avoided so fundamental an objection to their argument, hoping the reader wouldn't know of it or think about it. Instead, this writer concedes the point that much of the problem predates the events she criticizes. She even notes the data that challenge her position. But watch how she turns the reader back to her argument by throwing the weight of the objection behind her plea for environmental cleanup. With judo-like grace she turns an apparent weakness into a strength.

Qualification

A related strategy for strengthening an argument is to qualify, or reduce the scope of, a given claim. Qualification can make an argument more precise, more accurate, and more persuasive by narrowing the scope of objections that can be made to it. In an essay about global warming, for instance, the writer initially made a very broad claim: "Global warming is bad for everybody." As she developed her ideas, she chose a more qualified argument:

> Not that global warming will be bad for everybody everywhere. In some parts of the world—Scandinavia, Russia, North America—increases in average temperatures are likely to make more land available for agriculture. A 2002 United Nations report suggests that agricultural production in these regions is likely to increase substantially. But as the same report makes clear, while these relatively rich areas may benefit, poor countries—and billions of people—will suffer greatly from climate change.

By narrowing her claim, the writer focuses attention on the strongest part of her argument.

6 Using Sources

LIKE MOST WRITING done in the professional world, college essays are examples of persuasive writing. To persuade, essays must offer evidence for their claims, and one of the most standard forms of evidence is a source. There are two kinds of sources: primary and secondary. Primary sources are the raw material—things like literary texts, government documents, survey data, or experimental results—that academic work explores. Secondary sources provide a context—"the literature," or what other scholars have already said about a topic—that helps make sense of the data from primary sources. You might say that primary sources are the *what* of scholarship, while secondary sources are the *so what*. In academic writing, skill in handling both kinds of sources is essential.

An inexperienced or careless scholar decides what and how he will argue early on, not anticipating either to be changed much by his research. He gathers source material aimlessly—a library book or two here, an internet search there, perhaps a few quoted passages from an assigned text—and then uses whatever he has turned up, without worrying too much about its quality or usefulness. This is not the way to win over your reader. An experienced scholar, by contrast, crafts her argument while patiently exploring sources. She realizes that for any topic she cares to study, from acid rain to zydeco, there are sources, some especially influential and important. When a writer has systematically gathered good source material and let it shape her argument, she is much more likely to gain the reader's sympathetic interest. We like reading such works because they make us feel like we're listening to a sharp and lively conversation of ideas:

> Ever since Marshall Sahlins published his influential book *Stone Age Economics* in 1960, social anthropologists have been inclined to view traditional societies as living in an ecological Garden of Eden. (Robin Dunbar, *The Trouble with Science*)

> In a now famous put-down of Kauffman's ideas, John Maynard Smith once described them, somewhat harshly, as "fact-free science." (Paul Davies, *The Fifth Miracle*)

> While Faludi is extremely convincing about the breadth and depth of the
> backlash against feminism, she casts the media as all bad, and she sug-
> gests that this kind of backlash is relatively recent. Neither point is true.
> (Susan Douglas, *Where the Girls Are*)

Such "conversation" is a natural and integral part of good scholarship.
New scholarship builds on old—sometimes to support, sometimes to
modify, sometimes to question or even refute. It never exists in a vacuum.
If a scholar writes as though a field of inquiry has sprung full-blown from
her own head, ignores an important text, or uses inferior sources uncritically, she invites skepticism about the quality of her work. This chapter
offers three short lessons in using sources: winning your audience's trust,
weaving sources into your argument, and quoting effectively (for more
extensive advice, see Harvey).

Winning Your Audience's Trust

Academic readers have certain basic expectations about sources. Violate
the following expectations and you put your reader on guard. Meet them
and you begin to win your reader's trust, making him more receptive to
your argument.

Readers Expect Quality Sources

Needless to say, not all sources are equally credible. Peer-reviewed
publications carry more weight than popular magazines. Some journals
and academic presses are more prestigious than others. Newer sources are
more up-to-date, as a rule of thumb, than older ones—though some older
sources and scholars achieve a kind of enduring authority, and no source
should be regarded uncritically simply because it is new. Some literary
editions and translations are more scholarly and reliable than others.
As for the internet, it must be treated with great care because there is no
quality control for what gets posted online; not only is getting information from the internet like drinking from a fire hose, but there's no
assurance that what comes out is safe to drink. In all of this, of course,
undergraduate students are at an immense disadvantage. How to com-
pensate for lack of experience? There are three simple remedies. First,
take a short course at your college library on how to conduct research.

Among other things, you'll learn how to use discipline-specific, subscription-only references—a filter that will help you limit your search to creditable sources. Second, know precisely what your teacher expects for an assignment—what kinds of sources, how many, and how scholarly or popular they may be. If necessary, ask your instructor. Asking is a sign of seriousness. Finally, take advantage of two useful guides: textbooks, which cite the most important literature on a given topic in bibliographies; and scholarly journals, which include lots of reviews of current literature.

Readers Expect Accuracy

When quoting a source this means getting the words exactly right: *verbatim et literatim* ("word for word, and letter for letter"), as the Latin proverb has it. Misspelling your own name on the title page is bad, but not as bad as a typo in a quotation. Accuracy also means summarizing sources fairly and not pulling fragments out of context without adequate explanation.

Readers Expect Careful Attribution

Drawing on other people's ideas is natural and inevitable in academic writing—but you must acknowledge the borrowing. Taking material from another work without acknowledgment is plagiarism, a form of theft and fraud that academics punish severely—among other reasons, because it strikes at the heart of their vocation. Plagiarism includes quoting material without signaling it as such, passing off someone else's idea as your own, and imitating the words or structure of a passage without citation (this last one means that slight changes in wording are not enough to avoid a charge of plagiarism). Even respected scholars can damage their reputations if they are discovered to have been sloppy in attributing material taken from other writers. The point of citations is to make it possible for your reader to check your work. Cite your sources according to the standards in the particular discipline for which you are writing. (The Appendix shows how to cite according to three common formats— CMOS, MLA, and APA.)

  Not everything needs to be cited. Don't cite familiar facts or common judgments:

Shakespeare was born in 1564.

The Earth orbits the sun at a distance of 93 million miles.

Many people have argued that there was a conspiracy to assassinate President John F. Kennedy.

But as you give more specific information, citations become necessary:

Shakespeare was born in 1564 in Stratford-upon-Avon, to a family originally from Arden (Levi 2, 8).

I'll be blunt. Plagiarism is vile but disturbingly common, especially with the rise of the internet as a word market. If appeals to virtue, education, and your mom—"Just because everyone does it doesn't make it right"—aren't enough to keep you honest, let me invoke the strongest motive of all, self-interest. Apart from the immediate risk of failing, probation, and expulsion, plagiarism creates a paper trail that even years later may reappear to cause harm and shame. Every so often one reads about some rising star whose career is cut short by the revelation of long-ago academic fraud. At the least, avoid plagiarism for prudential reasons.

Weaving Sources into Your Prose

How do you weave sources into your writing gracefully? One common way is to use the punch-line technique (see Chapter 3). Start your sentence with set-up information that identifies the text and/or author, and then state the argument of the text itself. Here's a nice example from Robin Dunbar's *The Trouble with Science*:

In his book *Contemporary Animal Learning Theory*, psychologist Tony Dickinson points out that there are two ways animals might store information about their experiences.

Why is this an example of a punch line? Because the "punch"—the new or detailed information—comes at the end of the sentence, after the "that," while the first part serves to set it all up. Dunbar begins the sentence by referring to a book, naming it, naming the author, and identifying the author's academic area. With those four pieces of information deployed, Dunbar is ready to tell us what the cited author actually said.

There are many other good ways to refer to a source. The following variations assume an in-text citation style, such as MLA or APA (see the Appendix for more information):

> Some have argued that prosperity depends on the degree of trust within a society (Fukuyama 1996).

> Fukuyama (1996) argues that the level of prosperity in a society depends on the level of trust.

> In his 1996 book, Fukuyama argues that trust is essential to the development of prosperous societies.

In-text author citations like these serve to flag sources without bogging the reader down with extraneous information in the body of the essay. They make it easier for readers to speed through your writing. Inexperienced academic writers sometimes neglect the author(s) and cite the title of the article, like this:

> The article "The Nature of Athlete Leadership" explores the nature of leadership on athletic teams, including how team leaders are perceived by other athletes.

Since the list of references is alphabetized by author, it's more helpful to your reader to cite the authors:

> Loughead, Hardy, and Eys (2006) explore the nature of leadership on athletic teams, including how team leaders are perceived by other athletes.

When citing several sources in a passage, one challenge is how to weave them together. An easy technique is to start a citation with a signal phrase that helps connect the new source to what has come before:

> On the other hand, Smith and Jimenez (2001) question whether this kind of self-monitoring really occurs.

> Supporting this view, Taylor (1961) famously argued that Hitler was opportunistic rather than strategic, and essentially stumbled into the Second World War.

By themselves, "on the other hand" and "supporting this view" don't make much sense. But in the context of a paper, we can see how they would serve to connect sources, creating a sense of interplay among them. Readers appreciate these little connectors.

When you want to signal your reader to evaluate a source in a particular way, one nice technique is to use an evaluative adverb. Scott Bravmann, in *Queer Fictions of the Past*, uses "forcefully" to suggest that his cited text is particularly effective:

> Recently, Jackie Goldsby has forcefully reminded us of the importance of racial analysis to gay and lesbian political, theoretical, and historical work. . . .

A complication in making sense of sources is that the source itself has its own tone. If a source is sardonic or ironic, for instance, and this will not be obvious from context in your essay, make the source's tone clear to your reader:

Original	Revision
Kinsley refers to the press secretary's "genius."	Kinsley refers sardonically to the press secretary's "genius."

In academic writing in the humanities and social sciences, sources rarely "prove" anything. Yet student writers often use this word, as if to establish by force of will that "proof" has been achieved. Academic readers in these areas don't, by and large, expect proof. They expect a well-reasoned and well-supported argument, and usually prefer arguments that include shades of gray as well as black and white. Here are some verbs that, in an academic setting at least, tend to persuade better than *prove*:

questions	argues	analyzes
explores	attacks	supports
disagrees	suggests	notes
shows	indicates	considers
attests to	argues for	underscores
testifies to	calls into question	complicates

Here's an example of how such words can supply a more measured academic tone:

Original	Revision
This proves that Yeats was a fervent Irish nationalist.	This testifies to Yeats's fervent Irish nationalism.

Quoting Effectively

This section presents some basic do's and don'ts of good quoting. It will be especially useful for writing in the humanities and the social sciences, where direct quotation is common.

Clarity

Most mistakes in quoting stem from carelessness with respect to clarity. A writer, reading through a whole text and deciding what to draw out for her essay, knows the context within which a particular passage makes sense. But a reader sees only the passage placed before him, out of context. Any loose threads, like a pronoun whose antecedent lies outside the quoted excerpt, will confuse a reader. In the following example, the original passage implies that Marx and Engels are talking about capitalism, which in a general sense they are. But in the source (a passage from the *Communist Manifesto*), Marx and Engels are talking about a particular economic class within capitalism, the bourgeoisie). This imprecision must be cleared up, as in the revision:

Original	Revision
Capitalism, Marx and Engels said, is different: "for exploitation, veiled by religious and political illusions, it has substituted naked, shameless, direct, brutal exploitation."	The modern bourgeoisie, Marx and Engels said, differs from previous oppressors: "for exploitation, veiled by religious and political illusions, it has substituted naked, shameless, direct, brutal exploitation."

Students often quote too much. It's better to break a source text into pieces and only use what you really need, as long as you're fair to the original meaning and fit the fragment grammatically into your sentence:

> Marius von Senden, reviewing every published case over a three-hundred-year period in his classic book *Space and Sight* (1932), concluded that every newly sighted adult sooner or later came to a "motivation crisis"—and that not every patient gets through it. (Oliver Sacks, *An Anthropologist on Mars*)

> Manchester's portrait of Churchill is complex. He calls him "a quaint survivor of Britain's past" but also "one of history's great originals" (3, 6).

> Adam Smith argued that capitalism benefited society not because of altruism but because "an invisible hand" linked the interests of the individual and society.

Note how these examples treat a quoted fragment like any other word or phrase to be fitted into the sentence. A quoted adjective is just an adjective; a quoted noun is just a noun.

Introducing Quotations

Introduce quotations concisely:

Original	Revision
In *The Prince*, Machiavelli says that the general requirement of a prince is to "endeavor to avoid those things which would make him the object of hatred and contempt" (64).	In *The Prince*, Machiavelli says that a prince should "endeavor to avoid those things which would make him the object of hatred and contempt" (64).

Experienced writers often economize by introducing a quotation with a colon attached to an existing statement, rather than writing a special introduction:

Original	Revision
The tension builds when Brutus accuses Cassius of accepting bribes. He states, "Let me tell you, Cassius, you yourself / Are much condemned to have an itching palm, / To sell and mart your offices for gold. . . ." (*JC* 4.3.9–11).	The tension builds when Brutus accuses Cassius of accepting bribes: "Let me tell you, Cassius, you yourself / Are much condemned to have an itching palm, / To sell and mart your offices for gold. . . ." (*JC* 4.3.9–11).

If a quotation consists of one or more complete sentences, introduce it with a colon or a comma. Here are some examples of each form:

Introduction with a Colon	Introduction with a Comma
Afterward he recalled the scene:	Afterward he recalled,
She professed astonishment:	She said,
Mill poses a question:	Mill asks,
Mill asks a question:	

An elegant trick is to insert the source within the quotation. This device forces the reader to pause, so you can shine a spotlight precisely where you want:

"Opinion," the old king emphasizes, "did help me to the crown" (*1H4* 3.2.42–47).

Long Quotations

Long quotations are treated differently from short ones. Set off a long quotation from your text, indenting on the left. Do not put quotation marks around a set-off or block quotation. In American academic style a colon is generally used to introduce a block quotation. See the Appendix for precise details on formatting long quotations for CMOS, MLA, and APA.

Modifying Quotations

Sometimes it's advisable to change a quotation slightly, either to make it fit grammatically, to explain or clarify a term, or to emphasize something. Here's how to make these changes.

When part of a quotation appears in italics, you need to make clear whether the emphasis is yours or the author's:

> Locke argues that every individual in the state of nature has a right to enforce the laws of nature: "the *execution* of the law of nature is, in that state, put into every man's hand . . ." (9, emphasis in the original).

> Wollstonecraft insists women cannot be excluded from access to education: "*truth must be common to all*, or it will be inefficacious with respect to its influence on general practice" (86, emphasis added).

To explain a missing antecedent or add anything else (such as a definition of an unfamiliar term), use brackets:

> Wollstonecraft does not want to reverse the sexual balance of power, but to move away from domination altogether: "I do not wish them [women] to have power over men; but over themselves" (156).

Another way to clear up a confusing word is to introduce the quotation with an eye to these loose ends:

> Wollstonecraft wants women to strive for autonomy, not domination: "I do not wish them to have power over men; but over themselves" (156).

Note that eighteenth-century usage permitted a semicolon where we would require a comma. The author does not correct this when quoting Wollstonecraft. Use your judgment about what to modify and what to leave alone. If you wish to correct the source text, insert the correction in brackets: [,]. Or mark the mistake with the word *sic* (Latin for "thus" or "so") in brackets: "The school's motto, *e pluribus unam* [*sic*], hardly inspired confidence." (*Sic* is also sometimes used to call the reader's attention to some peculiar or notable word or phrase in a quotation.)

6 Using Sources

Ellipsis

An academic writer may use whatever pieces of a source text he wishes. However, deletions within a quoted passage must be indicated by an ellipsis. (Naturally one is not allowed to change the meaning of the original in any material sense.) If you cut less than a full sentence, use the three-dot ellipsis, with spaces around the dots:

> In his *History of Florence*, Machiavelli summed up the situation tersely: "The evil . . . which external powers could not effect, was brought about by those within." (Michael Levey, *Florence: A Portrait*)

If the deleted portion of the quotation includes a sentence's terminal punctuation (the punctuation at the end of the sentence), or if you are using the quotation to end a sentence in your essay, add a fourth dot, representing the period. You must also use the four-dot ellipsis if you leave out a sentence or more from the quoted source. Make sure that what you do quote consists of grammatically complete sentences before and after the ellipsis:

> There is not a man beneath the canopy of heaven, that does not know that slavery is wrong *for him*. . . . At a time like this, scorching irony, not convincing argument, is needed (Douglass 34, emphasis in the original).

The reason for an ellipsis is to notify your reader that there are words missing from the quotation. If this is obvious, you don't need the dots:

Wrong	Right
Politicians and conquerors, Voltaire said, were ". . . celebrated villains."	Politicians and conquerors, Voltaire said, were "celebrated villains."

Punctuating Quotations

For punctuating quotations American usage is fairly simple: commas and periods go inside the quotation marks (by convention rather than for any rational reason), and all other punctuation marks go outside. If, however, these other punctuation marks are part of the original quotation, then you put them inside the quotation marks:

"What is it," Nietzsche asked, "that I especially find utterly unendurable?" (917).

With in-text quotations, the parenthetical citation (assuming you're using such a style) comes before the terminal punctuation (even if you have to invent a period, as above). With set-off quotations, the parenthetical comes after the terminal punctuation.

Quoting Poetry and Drama

You can quote up to three lines of poetry by incorporating the quotation within your text. Denote separate lines by using a slash with a space on each side (/):

> Gray imagines what those buried in the churchyard might have achieved, had they but had the opportunity: "Some mute inglorious Milton here may rest, / Some Cromwell, guiltless of his country's blood" (47–48).

If you quote more than three lines, set them off using the same formats as with other set-off quotations. You also need to imitate the poem's layout, which means attention to line indentations. If you begin quoting in the middle of a line of verse, convey this with extra indentation and an ellipsis. The ellipsis follows the same format as for prose quotations, except that if you skip one or more whole lines of verse, denote this with a line of spaced periods about the same length as the line of verse. Citations of poetry give line numbers, not pages.

If you quote from a play, incorporate the quotation within your text if it has just one speaker and is three lines or fewer in length. You will need to know if you're quoting verse or prose, since both occur in plays. If prose, treat the quote as any other quotation. If verse, follow the guidelines above for quoting poetry within your text. In either case, the citation identifies act, scene, and line rather than page:

> Finally, Antony rises to deliver his famous funeral oration: "Friends, Romans, countrymen, lend me your ears; / I come to bury Caesar, not to praise him. / The evil that men do lives after them; The good is oft interrèd with their bones" (*JC* 3.2.73–76).

If the excerpt has more than three lines, set off the quotation, following the guidelines for set-off poetry or prose.

Finally, if you quote a passage with more than one speaker, set off the quotation, identify the speakers, and reproduce the spatial arrangement of the printed lines:

Caesar: Welcome to Rome.
Antony: Thank you.
Caesar: Sit.
Antony: Sit, sir.
Caesar: Nay then.

        [They sit] (2.1.28)

Quotations within Quotations

If the main quotation has marks around it, mark the inner quotation with single quotation marks. But if the main quotation is a set-off quotation, mark the inner quotation with double quotation marks.

Emphasis with Quotation Marks

Do not use quotation marks merely to emphasize words in their normal sense. Not this, unless you're trying to be funny:

Tonight's dining-hall menu is "special."

Use quotation marks to point to a word whose meaning is under consideration:

Rousseau's "freedom" is difficult for Americans to comprehend.

But if you use other words to point to the word, skip the quotation marks:

Wrong	Right
Rousseau's concept of "freedom" is difficult for Americans to comprehend.	Rousseau's concept of freedom is difficult for Americans to comprehend.

Use quotation marks to flag words used sardonically or ironically:

> The "impartial" jury took less than twenty minutes to find the defendant guilty.

Adjectives like *supposed, so-called, would-be, ostensible,* and *putative* (or their adverbial forms) make such quotation marks unnecessary:

Wrong	Right
The ostensibly "impartial" jury took less than twenty minutes to find the defendant guilty.	The ostensibly impartial jury took less than twenty minutes to find the defendant guilty.

Use quotation marks for translations of foreign words:

> Legend has it that as the seventy-year-old Galileo rose from his knees, he muttered under his breath, *"Eppure si muove"* ("Yet it moves").

Certain scholarly disciplines, notably philosophy, use single quotation marks to denote a term used as a term:

> 'Freedom' is an ambiguous term.

7 Paragraphs

THUS FAR WE have considered essays mainly at the level of individual words and sentences (though in Chapter 3 we considered flow from one sentence to the next). Now we turn our attention to larger structural elements, starting with paragraphs.

The Function of Paragraphs

What are paragraphs? In essence, a form of punctuation—and like other forms of punctuation, they are meant to make written material easier to read. Visually, paragraphs are blocks of text marked with an indented first line (usually a half-inch indent; for college essays it's better to indent than use a blank line). Functionally, paragraphs represent pieces of an argument. Lincoln's Gettysburg Address, for instance, consists of just three short paragraphs: the first about the past, the second the present, and the third the future. Lincoln, a great communicator, chose this simple structure to reinforce his speech's intention. He wished to evoke in the minds of his audience an emotional link between America's founding, the present conflict, and the enduring values for which he said Americans were fighting. The harmony of the design helped make this the most famous speech in our nation's history.

Of course there are countless ways to structure arguments, and thus countless ways to arrange an essay into paragraphs. But any sound arrangement requires the writer to do three things: (1) understand your own argument (*What do I wish to say to the reader?*); (2) decide on a sensible way to lay out this argument (*From the reader's perspective, what piece-by-piece arrangement of supporting and explanatory material will best illuminate the argument?*); and (3) have the discipline to stick to this structure (*Does each paragraph—and each sentence—fit with my plan?*). (In practice there's a fourth requirement—willingness to modify your design as the need arises.) The most important thing to remember is that paragraphs are there for your reader's benefit, not because of some abstract rule of composition.

Is there an optimal length for paragraphs? In one sense, no. Whether we count by words, lines, or sentences, there is considerable variation in good writing, depending on several factors: the nature of the written text, the academic discipline, the writer's predilections, and the shifting needs of the argument for more or less detail and development. But if we keep in mind that texts are divided into paragraphs for the convenience of the reader, and that readers find great undifferentiated blocks of text highly inconvenient and inaccessible, we begin to get a sense of the ordinary "right" length. Paragraphs that typically exceed a page aren't doing much to make a text easier to read. It turns out that good academic writers typically divide a page of text into two to four paragraphs. (Some writers use the visual breaks created by set-off quotations somewhat like paragraph marks. New paragraphs may be less frequent, but there will still tend to be two to four blocks of text per page.) In undergraduate writing, this means that typical paragraphs are likely to be somewhere in the neighborhood of 100 to 200 words, or 8 to 15 lines, long. (For reference, an average double-spaced page of 12-point text has about 300 to 350 words, and around 23 lines.)

But dividing text into two to four paragraphs per page won't help the reader much if these divisions appear arbitrary. Paragraphs break up not only the look of a text; they also break up the argument into a series of topics or steps. Paragraphs help us see an argument as a logical sequence of steps. From the writer's perspective it is better to pay attention to this sequence than to the length of any given step. As H. W. Fowler observed, "The paragraph is essentially a unit of thought, not of length" (434).

What, then, constitutes a "unit of thought"? It depends on the assignment, on the topic, on the step-by-step unfolding of the argument. Occasionally a unit of thought may be expressed in a single sentence. Here, for instance, the acclaimed neurologist and writer Oliver Sacks uses a one-sentence paragraph, as simple and graceful as an elegy, to end his discussion of a young autistic man's experiences with music:

It was as if, for a brief time, he had become truly alive.

More typically, the formulaic five-paragraph essay on which many high-school students cut their teeth has a sturdy "unit of thought" paragraph structure: an introductory paragraph with a thesis statement, three body paragraphs that each provide one piece of supporting material, and a concluding paragraph. College writing adds detail and complexity but keeps this basic design. The opening and concluding sections of a college essay are likely to expand into more than one paragraph each (and in a thesis or a book, they become whole chapters). The three-paragraph body grows into a more complex structure, because you cover more material or explore it in greater depth (or both). Your argument will grow to include more elements, such as a consideration of contrary viewpoints (with a rebuttal or concession or both). You will delve into secondary sources. Brief summaries broaden into more nuanced, critically informed discussions. The upshot is that in college you may tackle the same topic you once dispatched in a two-page, five-paragraph essay, but now it may take you twenty pages and fifty or so paragraphs.

Opening Sentences

An opening sentence tells the reader what a paragraph is about. The opening sentence is also usually the topic sentence, or the sentence that summarizes the paragraph, but there is no rule that says paragraphs must have topic sentences, or that they must come at the beginning. Still, the beginning is the natural place to learn where a paragraph is going:

> When we see a play, what is it that we see?

> A popular audience for science, and for technology, blossomed in Europe and America in the 19th century.

> The process of growth and change in evolution is chaotic and filled with conflict.

> Historians have judged the "October Days" as the single most significant activity undertaken by women during the Revolution. (Marilyn Yalom, *Blood Sisters*)

Sometimes a topic is deployed across two sentences:

> The third and final area of Theban expansion was by sea in the Aegean. Here again the enemy was Athens.

The opening sentence is also where the reader can see how the paragraph connects to what has come before. Some of the techniques we studied in Chapter 3—in particular, characters, pointers, and conjunctions—merit a second look at this point. They can help produce opening sentences that fit well together. First, let's look at consistent characters—in this example, *model*:

> The model of the iterated Prisoner's Dilemma is much less restricted than it may at first appear. . . . ¶ The model does assume that the choices are made simultaneously and with discrete time intervals. . . . (Robert Axelrod, *The Evolution of Cooperation*)

In the next example, we look at eight successive opening sentences (all but the first are also topic sentences). The repetition of a key term, *constancy*, lets the reader follow the developing argument:

> "Were man but constant, he were perfect." . . . ¶ Constancy is a superhuman virtue, possible only in the undecaying realms above the moon. . . . ¶ Constancy is central to Shakespeare's vision of human harmony. . . . ¶ This notion is fundamental to all of the plays. . . . ¶ The ideal of constancy functions in the comedies as a moral standard. . . . ¶ Constancy is rare indeed in actuality. . . . ¶ Julia's constancy is cast in the Griselde mold. . . . ¶ Constancy is magical, however, only in female characters. . . . (Marilyn French, *Shakespeare's Division of Experience*)

A second way to link paragraphs is to use pointing words such as relative adjectives in the new paragraph's opening sentence:

> This outcome seems to support Kuhn's argument.

> Lincoln was very careful in framing these parallels. (Garry Wills, *Lincoln at Gettysburg*)

Pronouns, however, are one kind of pointing word not so often used in opening sentences. Good writers often restate an antecedent noun in an opening sentence, for emphasis and clarity:

Original	Revision
He never forgot this lesson.	Marlowe never forgot this lesson.

The third common technique for opening sentences that help connect a paragraph to the previous paragraph is to use conjunctions and conjunctive adverbs, in all the varieties listed in Chapter 3:

Warfare was basic to the Hellenistic world, in two ways. First, the legiti-
macy of the Hellenistic king rested in part on his military prestige. . . . ¶
Secondly, the scope of warfare was greatly enlarged. . . . (*The Oxford
History of the Classical World*)

Still, Greenleaf believed his vision of ethical leadership was practical.

The slaves also turned their satire against themselves. (Eugene Genovese,
Roll, Jordan, Roll)

Let's look at one extended example. Here is a sequence (from Robin
Dunbar's *The Trouble with Science*) that shows how ten successive paragraphs begin:

1. ¶ The business of hypothesis-testing is neither easy nor straight-
   forward. . . .

2. ¶ What, then, defines a good theory? In his book *The Rationality
   of Science*, the philosopher William Newton-Smith lists eight key
   features. . . .

3. ¶ Newton-Smith is specifically concerned to counter the anti-
   rationalist views advocated by Kuhn and Feyerabend. . . .

4. ¶ Newton-Smith argues that the anti-rationalists are trying to foist
   much too grand a goal on to science. . . .

5. ¶ On the other hand, Newton-Smith is equally critical of rationalists like Popper and Lakatos, arguing that they have also taken too
   strict a view of scientists at work. . . .

6. ¶ This pragmatic line has, in fact, been argued by other philoso-
   phers of science. . . .

7. ¶ Rescher argues that this is the only rational way to proceed if we
   wish to live and survive in the real world. . . .

8. ¶ The philosopher Nicholas Maxwell wants to go further by insist-
   ing that there are even stronger grounds for justifying modern
   scientific practice. . . .

9. ¶ Maxwell calls this "aim-oriented empiricism" and contrasts it with the "standard empiricism" of conventional philosophy of science. . . .

10. ¶ The only possible recourse open to a relativist at this point is to argue that the success of a theory does not guarantee its truth. . . .

How many links can you find? I count at least twenty.

Designing Paragraphs

Remember that paragraphs represent units of thought within an argument. Such units of thought might include explanation, example, description, narration, definition, comparison, contrast, or analysis (see also Weston). A good writer will design a paragraph to match its function. A paragraph of examples, for instance, is basically a list, with everything that implies about symmetry and parallelism. A description should be composed in a manner that accords with what you're describing—for instance, work through a visual description with some sort of spatial order, say from left to right or foreground to background. Narration, naturally, tends to unfold chronologically. Failing to match form to function is one of the more common weaknesses of student writing. Let's look at some examples of how paragraphs should match form to function.

Example. One of the most common purposes for paragraphs is to offer evidence by way of examples. A paragraph may focus on a single detailed example. Or, as here, a writer may provide multiple examples:

> A new division of labor between suppliers and customers is reinventing industries. In Spartanburg, for example, Symtech Systems and Technology no longer simply sells equipment to its manufacturing customers. It designs and oversees their manufacturing processes as they use the equipment. In Aberdeen, Scotland, oil company customers such as BP (British Petroleum) and Conoco work with suppliers such as engineering firm Brown & Root to rethink the supply chain. (Rosabeth Moss Kanter, *World Class*)

> Often place-names arise from mishearings or misunderstandings— notably the West Indies, which of course have nothing to do with India.

They simply reflect Columbus's startling inability to determine which hemisphere he was in. Yucatán in Mexico means "What?" or "What are you saying?"—the reply given by the natives to the first Spanish conquistadors to fetch up on their shores. The term *Dutch* is similarly based on a total misapprehension. It comes from Deutsch, or German, and the error has been perpetuated in the expression Pennsylvania Dutch—who are generally not Dutch at all but German. (Bill Bryson, *The Mother Tongue*)

Description. In crafting a description of something—a picture, a building, a scene, an event, or anything else—you have lots of choices. If the thing to be described is complex, it's important to describe it in a way that helps the reader put the pieces together: right to left, bottom to top, first to last, big to small, foreground to background, or whatever pattern fits the material, your purpose, and the reader's expectations (unless surprise is part of your design). A good writer arranges material in a way that suits his theme. Here, for instance, Paul Fussell describes World War I trenches:

> There were normally three lines of trenches. The front-line trench was anywhere from fifty yards or so to a mile from its enemy counterpart. Several hundred yards behind it was the support trench line. And several hundred yards behind that was the reserve line. There were three kinds of trenches: firing trenches, like these; communication trenches, running roughly perpendicular to the line and connecting the three lines; and "saps," shallower ditches thrust out into No Man's Land, providing access to forward observation posts, listening posts, grenade-throwing posts, and machine gun positions. The end of a sap was usually not manned all the time: night was the favorite time for going out. Coming up from the rear, one reached the trenches by following a communication trench sometimes a mile or more long. It often began in a town and gradually deepened. By the time pedestrians reached the reserve line, they were well below ground level. (Paul Fussell, *The Great War and Modern Memory*)

The paragraph begins with description of a static scene and then shifts to a more dynamic description that incorporates movement and people. Fussell arranges his description spatially in two ways, at least: first he ranges across the parallel and perpendicular lines of the trenches; then he imagines approaching and descending into the trenches.

Description begins with analysis, or the breaking of a whole into constituent pieces. A good writer arranges the pieces so that the reader can see how they fit and "move." In highly descriptive fields like art history, this kind of writing is an art unto itself:

> The Crucifixion (fig. 172) is shorn of all elements of pain and terror, save only for the grief of the angels. The still figure on the Cross looks almost pityingly at Mary and St. John seated on the ground below. The curves of their bodies, following those of the quatrefoil, are completed by those of the angels. All the curves are subsumed in the concave lines of Christ's arms. A typically Ghibertian composition always shows a counterpoise of the compositional elements and the directional flow of rhythms that produces a perfect and abstract unity. In the case of the Crucifixion, the opposition and swing of the rhythms raise this unity to the level of an unearthly harmony around the sacrificed Christ. (Frederick Hartt, *History of Italian Renaissance Art*)

Narration. Narration describes actions unfolding over time. Clear narration usually follows chronological order. Here, the writer narrates a series of events and then draws a general conclusion:

> Britain first tried to reverse its decline and decay by depending primarily on what are called demand-side measures, to no avail. Then it joined the European Economic Community, to no avail. Then it switched to what are called supply-side measures, again to no avail. No matter what Britain has tried, it has continued in the grip of unrelenting decline, much like any other faded, fabled empire of the distant past before people had economic theories and instructions and statistics to guide them. (Jane Jacobs, *Cities and the Wealth of Nations*)

Definition. There are a great many ways to define things. But one of the first things college students are expected to learn is that terms and ideas are often not amenable to conclusive definition. A definition that seems satisfactory so long as you don't think about it often turns out to be problematic when you start asking questions (blame it on Socrates). To the simple question, "What is leadership?," for instance, it turns out there is no agreed-upon answer. An academic writer, nevertheless, is expected to try to bring some measure of order to complex material:

> What is leadership? There is no universal definition. Scholars have sought to answer this question in several different ways: by focusing on leaders' traits or behaviors, by analyzing the different kinds of tasks leaders

perform, by looking at the relationship between leaders and followers, and by seeing whether leadership differs across different cultures.

Here, in a much more sophisticated example, a writer explores an everyday phenomenon, so that a simple question—"What is color?"—no longer seems simple at all:

> Color is not a trivial subject but one that has compelled, for hundreds of years, a passionate curiosity in the greatest artists, philosophers, and natural scientists. The young Spinoza wrote his first treatise on the rainbow; the young Newton's most joyous discovery was the composition of white light; Goethe's great color work, like Newton's, started with a prism; Schopenhauer, Young, Helmholtz, and Maxwell, in the last century, were all tantalized by the problem of color; and Wittgenstein's last work was his *Remarks on Colour*. And yet most of us, most of the time, overlook its great mystery. Through such a case as Mr. I's we can trace not only the underlying cerebral mechanisms or physiology but the phenomenology of color and the depth of its resonance and meaning for the individual. (Oliver Sacks, "The Case of the Colorblind Painter")

Sections

Some arguments lend themselves to being broken into larger units than paragraphs. Such sections may be marked in several ways: with numbers or asterisks centered above each section, with white space, or with headings. Avoid breaking short essays into sections.

8 Beginnings and Endings

IN EARLIER CHAPTERS we focused on words and sentences; in Chapter 7 we turned to paragraphs. Now we close with thoughts on the essay as a whole. A whole, Aristotle said in his *Poetics*, "is that which has a beginning, a middle, and an end." Aristotle hit on something basic. As the stylist Sheridan Baker put it a few years ago, "Build your essay in three parts. There really is no other way" (27). An essay tries to make a reader care about, accept, and remember your argument. The beginning grabs the reader's attention, prepares a context, and states the argument. The middle (or body) works through the argument step-by-step: giving examples, connecting the general and the particular, unfolding causal relationships, and using good supporting materials. The ending (or conclusion) repeats key points and sends the reader off feeling that she's learned something worthwhile.

Beginnings

The appropriate length for a beginning varies by discipline, assignment, and topic, but as a rule of thumb we can expect a good beginning to range from a single paragraph for a short essay, to perhaps a couple of pages for a long essay of twenty to twenty-five pages. (A book's introduction would be a whole chapter.) All good beginnings include a thesis statement, context, and a starting point.

A thesis statement is your argument in a nutshell. By contrast, a topic is what your essay is about: global warming, say, or the War of Jenkins's Ear, or Amazon.com. A common mistake is to state a topic and leave it at that: *This essay will look at Amazon.com.* Readers need more information. What are you going to say about your topic? What problem are you going to investigate? What is your argument? That's the point of a thesis statement: to distill your argument to a single sentence. With Amazon, you might end up with a thesis statement like this one: *Amazon.com is here to stay.*

Here's another topic presented as if it were a thesis statement:

> There is a common theme between Federalist essays 10 and 51: power.

So general a statement does little to help the reader. It lacks a *who-does-what* message. As the writer thought about how to turn "power" from a topic to an argument, she realized two things. First, that the more precise term "conflict" did a better job of capturing her topic than the broad "power." Second, that she was thinking about what arguments the Federalist essays made about this topic. These realizations shaped her revision, which serves as a *who-does-what* guide to her essay:

> Federalist 10 and 51 both see conflict as the gravest danger to popular government. But instead of trying to eliminate or suppress conflict, they suggest ways of harnessing its power.

Context

Depending on the expertise of your intended audience, you are likely to have to provide a context for your argument. In an essay about Amazon, for instance, you'd want to make sure your reader knew some of the broad outlines of the story of Amazon's origins, rise, and troubles—the rise and fall of the internet bubble and the collapse of many other dot-coms. Without giving all the details of your story in the beginning, create a frame within which your argument or story makes sense. Here's an example, from the introduction of a book on Islam:

> *Dar el-Islam*, the House of Islam, embraces nearly 900 million people of every race, from Senegal to China, from Nigeria to the Soviet Union, and more than two million Americans as well. All are Muslims, sharing common religious beliefs, but they vary widely in behavior. Most of them are not leftists or fanatics or revolutionaries or extremists. They cannot be stereotyped in the image of one race or one kind of political or social conduct. Certainly it is absurd to identify Islam with Arabs luxuriating in oil wealth. The vast majority of Muslims are not Arabs and not wealthy. . . . (Thomas W. Lippman, *Understanding Islam*)

Starting Points

Good writers usually start an essay with something small—a story, a quotation, an example, a question, a detail, or the like—that connects to something big, the argument to be pursued. For instance, Ian Tattersall begins his study of human origins (in *Becoming Human*) with the most famous images from prehistory, the cave paintings of southern Europe. Robin Dunbar begins a book about science with the following lines:

> In 1632 the Italian astronomer Galileo Galilei published his *Dialogue Concerning the Two Chief World Systems*. In doing so he inadvertently set in motion one of the greatest revolutions in the history of the human race. (*The Trouble with Science*)

Rosabeth Moss Kanter's *World Class: Thriving Locally in the Global Economy*, a book on globalization and its impact on local businesses and communities, begins thus:

> A friend who lives year-round on Martha's Vineyard recounts the questions his five-year-old son asked him while walking on the beach one day:
>
> "We live on an island, right?" Right, my friend replied.
>
> "We're surrounded by water, right?" Right again.
>
> Pause.
>
> "Are we connected to the world?"
>
> The answer to that question is, of course, yes.

Finally, here is how the scholar Hanna Fenichel Pitkin begins *Fortune Is a Woman*, a book on Machiavelli:

> Niccolò Machiavelli may well be the most political of all the great political theorists; and, like politics itself, Machiavelli horrifies and repels us, yet also attracts and fascinates. We do not know what to make of him, or how to think rightly about political life. We know that politics matters profoundly, perhaps more in our time than ever before; we suspect that somehow we have gotten it terribly wrong; but we feel powerless to change, or even fully to understand our situation. For me, thinking about politics and thinking about Machiavelli have become interconnected enterprises, each illuminating and obscuring the other. That is the reason for this book.

The author locates her subject, raises thorny problems about politics, and involves us, her readers—our thoughts, our feelings, and our fears—in her project. A powerful beginning.

The beginning of an essay also gives your reader a first impression of what you sound like. In general the most effective tone for college essays is one of reasoned argument and fair consideration of opposing viewpoints. It is fine to argue strenuously, but remember that the point is rational persuasion. If your essay sounds one-sided or narrow, you are less likely to achieve that goal. Consider the following two opening paragraphs. They treat the same topic, school choice (programs that provide public funding for children to attend private schools). The two versions reflect the same position—strong opposition to school choice—but make crucially different claims. The original is accusatory, while the revision sticks to school choice and its alleged effects:

Original	Revision
The school-choice movement is a racist scheme to weaken public education. School-choice advocates don't care about minorities, fairness, or even children. Instead, they want to use tax dollars to support conservative religious groups and increase the massive segregation of American society. School choice is nothing more than an attack on democracy and multiculturalism.	Among the most predictable consequences of implementing school-choice would be not a public school system strengthened by competition, but one further weakened by it. Tax dollars would go to support conservative religious groups and increase the massive segregation of American society. Minorities, fairness, and children would suffer too. But the ultimate victims would be multiculturalism and democracy itself.

The original paragraph attacks the sincerity and motives of school-choice advocates. The revision, by contrast, focuses on what the author thinks is wrong with the policy itself. This is not to say, of course, that motives may never be questioned. But accusations of bad faith or malicious motive are hard to establish; voiced as mere assertion they tend to undermine the persuasive power of an essay—except for those readers who already agree.

Let's look at another beginning marred by an ineffective tone. The paragraph comes from an essay that was, on the whole, well-written—full of strong verbs and clear statements. But in this opening paragraph the writer tried so hard to list all the key points that she forgot about verbs. The result is an inert sentence in the grip of the pompous style. The revision is truer to the rest of the essay:

Original	Revision
This paper will seek to analyze the privatization effort of Ukraine and come to a conclusion about the factors contributing to the lack of success of the attempt to reform and revive the troubled economy of the country.	In the early 1990s a newly independent Ukraine, seeking to reform and revive its troubled economy, embarked on a major privatization effort. The effort proved largely unsuccessful. This paper analyzes the privatization initiatives the Ukrainian government undertook, and the reasons for their failure.

Endings

What should an ending do? The common answer—summarize the argument—is correct as far as it goes. Here's a run-of-the-mill ending that does nothing more than summarize:

> Although Mark Antony seems like an unimportant character at the beginning of *Julius Caesar*, he develops into an extremely shrewd and powerful ruler who successfully utilizes Machiavellian strategies such as plotting political moves, gaining the acceptance of the common people, and never deferring war.

This conclusion is little more than a list of the points the essay covered. Better endings provide a measure of order and emphasis, encouraging the reader to look back on the whole argument, not just its various pieces. And the best endings manage to look outward—drawing some larger conclusion and pointing to a significant implication or an opportunity for further research. Good endings possess a paradoxical quality: a sense of closure combined with a suggestion of new spaces to explore. The revision of the above example reaches for such an effect:

> Mark Antony seems, at the beginning of *Julius Caesar*, a shallow and unimportant character. But by the end of the play he has been revealed as

bold, shrewd, and ambitious, the play's most thoroughly Machiavellian character. Has he changed—or has Shakespeare merely allowed us to see beneath his mask? And was his love for Caesar genuine, or opportunistic? Shakespeare poses these questions about Antony without providing easy answers. Contemplating Antony, we come to see *Julius Caesar* as a deeply political play, a play that challenges and teaches us about the nature of politics and the temptations of power.

Closing the Circle

Thy firmness makes my circle just,
And makes me end where I begun.
                    John Donne (1572–1631)

One of the best ways to end an essay is by *closing the circle*, or returning at the end to where you began. Return to the story, example, quotation, or the like that you used in your introduction. This imparts a sense of order, elegance, and control to an essay. Remembering how you started when you finish suggests you've been paying close attention to your argument: that makes your reader more inclined to do the same. Here's an example from an essay on Shakespeare's *Coriolanus*:

Beginning

"Boy of tears," Aufidius taunts the Roman general Coriolanus near the end of Shakespeare's play (5.6.100), and the vehemence of Coriolanus's response suggests that Aufidius has hit the mark: there is something childish and sad about this fiercely proud warrior.

Ending

By the end, Coriolanus has thrown away not only his old identity but his new one as well. The "boy of tears" is left with only his immature fury and sullen isolation. His final act of mercy leads not to reconciliation but to further suffering, loss, and death.

Another example comes from an essay about a visit to an isolated Caribbean island. The writer begins with a little detail that captures the island's isolation and slow pace: a tardy mail boat, which the writer will use to get to the island:

Beginning

The mail boat should have been here hours ago. From my stool in Blind Sonny Lloyd's tiny waterfront bar, I can see past a stand of coconut palms to the wooden deck where the boat was to have picked me up. (Tidwell E1)

At the end, the writer comes back to this opening image:

Ending

As it turns out, I'm the only passenger on the mail boat this time. I stash my gear in a tiny cabin and later recall something Percy had told me after our lobster dive as we waded ashore under the lavish Bahamian sun. "Think about what kind of world we'd have if every kid on the planet could grow up on an island like this. There'd be no more violence, mon. No more hatred. Just love for everybody. A big, big love."

If only Ragged Island could gobble up the rest of the world, in other words, instead of sliding slowly in the opposite direction. We could all be stranded together. Marooned as a way of life. The world as one big island.

And we wouldn't need mail boats any more. (Tidwell E8)

As these examples suggest, a skilled writer doesn't merely repeat what he said at the beginning. The trick is to echo the words or image with which you began while adding something that points beyond the text, that reaches out to the reader's world.

Last Thought

And so we come to our own ending. I hope that this little book has helped you better understand college writing. I hope that it has also helped you perceive the power and the beauty of words. Remember this: when you write something worth reading it won't be because you followed the rules and conventions (as important as those are if you wish to be taken seriously). It will be because you had something real to say, and said it with clarity and grace. "Words sing," the writer Leo Rosten once said. "They hurt. They teach. They sanctify. They were man's first, immeasurable feat of magic." There is indeed a wild magic in words. Reach, and see if you can grasp it.

Appendix

Document and Citation Formats

Generic Formats

As always, check with your teacher (or, even better, the course syllabus) to find out what her particular preferences are for every aspect of document preparation. Generally, essays should be printed in black ink on white 8.5 × 11 inch paper, and stapled in the upper-left corner. Common fonts include 12-point Times Roman and Arial.

In the days of typewriters and nonproportional fonts, it was common to put two spaces between sentences to improve readability. But today most teachers prefer just one space between sentences.

Italics or Underlining

Both *italics* and <u>underlining</u> convey emphasis and are used for the titles of books. If your teacher doesn't have a preference, use one or the other and be consistent. (*Nuts and Bolts* prefers italics.) Don't use bold face, except for headings of sections or figures. Use italics or underlining for foreign words or words you are pointing to as words:

> Machiavelli also uses *virtù* in its traditional sense of goodness or morality.

> *Yoga* and *yoke* derive from a common Sanskrit root.

Some foreign words have made it into common English usage and don't take italics. If you're unsure, consult a dictionary. Using italics for emphasis ("this is *extremely* important") should be avoided in academic writing.

Title and Identification

Your essay's title (usually between seven and fifteen words) should not be italicized or put in quotation marks (though if you are giving the title of a book or essay, or using a quotation in your title, then format those words accordingly). The title should be more than a bare-bones identifier (not "Essay #1" or "Essay on Management"). It should signal to the reader what your essay is about:

> Mysteries of State: An Absolute Concept and Its Late Medieval Origins
>
> "Hell Strives with Grace": Reflections on the Theme of Providence in Marlowe

Titles, especially in the humanities, often consist of two elements joined with a colon—typically, one of the elements is general, and the other more specific.

Corrections

Sometimes you will discover mistakes in a final draft, with no time to print a corrected version. In such cases you should strike through the mistake and write the correction above the line in question, marking the insertion point with a caret:

> *1945*
> The World Bank was established in ~~1947~~.
> ^

It's usually okay to turn in an essay with one or two such corrections.

CMOS, MLA, and APA Style Guide

This appendix furnishes a concise list of document and citation formats for three widely used academic styles: that of the University of Chicago Press's *Chicago Manual of Style* (known as CMOS, common in the humanities), that of the Modern Language Association (MLA, common in literature), and that of the American Psychological Association (APA, common in the social sciences).

CMOS citation style (from the *Chicago Manual of Style*, 17th edition) is widely used in history and in other disciplines within the humanities. CMOS actually includes two documentation styles, the notes and bibliography system and an author-date system similar to the APA and MLA styles. This style guide focuses on the notes and bibliography system, which requires the use of notes—either footnotes, at the bottom of each page, or endnotes, at the end of each section or at the end of the whole work. A popular companion guide for CMOS is Kate L. Turabian's *Manual for Writers of Research Papers, Theses, and Dissertations*, University of Chicago Press, 9th edition. It contains a number of slight modifications from the *Chicago Manual of Style* suitable to undergraduate papers.

The second citation style, MLA (from the Modern Language Association: see the *MLA Handbook*, 8th edition), is also widely used in the humanities. It requires the use of in-text citations rather than footnotes (though it allows the writer to make limited use of explanatory footnotes or endnotes).

The third common citation style, APA (from the American Psychological Association: see the *Publication Manual of the American Psychological Association*, 7th edition), is widely used in the social sciences. The APA also maintains a blog that provides some quasi-authoritative style guidance on evolving citation complexities (for instance, how to cite tweets or e-books) at https://apastyle.apa.org/blog. This Appendix includes guidance from the APA style blog to supplement the 7th edition of the APA manual.

For all three style formats, this guide lists basic document formats, plus recommended formats for the two pieces of a citation of a source: (1) the in-text citation or note, and (2) the reference at the end of the work. Because of changes from edition to edition, and because instructors may adhere to older editions or have their own preferences, do not be surprised if particular instructors have divergent requirements for their versions of these three common styles.

Basic Document Formats

CMOS   Margins: at least one inch, no more than one and one-half inches. Use an easy-to-read font (like Times New Roman), preferably in 12-point size, but at least 10 point. Double-space, except:

- Block quotations, captions, and table titles are single-spaced.
- Notes and bibliographic entries are single-spaced, with blank lines between.

CMOS recommends putting one space after periods and other end-of-sentence punctuation marks. Indent the first line of paragraphs one-half inch. Page numbers are placed at the top right or bottom center, half an inch from the edge of the page, using Arabic numbers. For student essays, it is customary to include the student's last name before the page number. Longer papers may take subheadings, which have blank lines above and below and should not end with periods. You may choose your own subhead style, but be consistent. Print your work on standard white 8.5 × 11 inch paper.

MLA   Use one-inch margins. Use an easy-to-read font (like Times New Roman) in 12-point size. Double-space. Insert one space after periods and other end-of-sentence punctuation marks. Indent the first line of paragraphs one-half inch, preferably using a tab, not spaces. Do not insert white space or blank lines between paragraphs. Create a header with your last name and then the page number in the top-right corner, one-half inch from the top and flush with the right margin. Do not use a page identifier like "p." Use italics for titles of longer works and for emphasis. Endnotes, if used, should be on a separate page (or pages) before the "Works Cited" page. This section is titled "Notes," with the title centered but otherwise not specially formatted. Print your work on standard white 8.5 × 11 inch paper.

APA   Use one-inch margins. Use an easy-to-read font (like Times New Roman) in 12-point size. Double-space. APA 7th edition recommends using one space after periods and other end-of-sentence punctuation marks. Indent the first line of paragraphs one-half inch. Do not insert white space or blank lines between paragraphs. Previously APA style required a running head flush left at the top of the page, but the 7th edition of APA style guide has eliminated the running head for student papers. Use italics for titles of longer works and for emphasis. APA discourages use of notes. For any footnotes, use your word processor's default note style, usually a slightly smaller font, and single-spaced. For extensive details on notes, consult the *APA Publication Manual*, 7th edition.

Quotations

CMOS   **Short quotations.** For quotations of fewer than five lines or 100 words, integrate the quotation into your body text and enclose it in quotation marks:

> After this, Jan Kott says, Fortinbras "smiles and is very pleased with himself."[4]

Long quotations. Quotations of more than four lines of prose or more than 100 words should be set off from the body text in a freestanding block. Quotation marks are not placed around the block quotation, which is single-spaced and starts on a new line, indented one-half inch from the left margin. If you're citing a single paragraph, the first line is not indented; but if you're citing multiple paragraphs, each subsequent first line is indented an extra one-half inch. When quoting two or more lines of verse, maintain original line breaks and keep layout close to the original. If you add words to a quotation, or alter a word to make the quoted passage fit grammatically in another sentence, put brackets around your words to indicate the addition. If you omit something from a quotation, indicate the deletion with an ellipsis, three periods preceded and followed by a space (. . .). (But generally avoid ellipses at the beginning or end of a quoted passage.) If you omit an entire line of verse from a quotation, indicate the omission with a line of periods stretching about the width of the verse. Adding or deleting words is permissible if necessary for clarity, as long as you don't alter the sense of the quoted passage, and as long as you flag the additions or deletions as described here.

MLA   Quotations, like other material, are double-spaced and presented in the same font as body text.

Short quotations. For quotations of four or fewer lines of prose, or three or fewer lines of poetry, integrate the quotation into your body text and enclose it in quotation marks. If, as is usually the case, a parenthetical citation comes at the end of a sentence or clause, punctuation follows the citation (with the exception that question and exclamation marks, if they are part of the quoted passage, should appear within the quotation marks):

> After this, Jan Kott says, Fortinbras "smiles and is very pleased with himself" (72).

Since short quotations from poetry (three or fewer lines) will be integrated into the body of your essay, mark the line breaks with a slash (/), preceded and followed by a space, between lines of verse:

> Lear tries to comfort Cordelia: "Come, let's away to prison.
> / We two alone will sing like birds i' th' cage" (5.3.9–10).

Long quotations. Quotes of more than four lines of prose, or more than three lines of verse, should be set off from the body text in a freestanding block, indented one inch from the left margin and starting on a new line. Quotation marks are not placed around a block quotation. If you're citing a single paragraph, the first line is not indented; but if you're citing multiple paragraphs, each first line is indented an extra one-quarter inch. One important difference from short quotations: for block quotations the parenthetical citation comes after the closing punctuation mark. When quoting verse, maintain original line breaks and keep layout close to the original.

If you add words to a quotation, or alter a word to make the quoted passage fit grammatically in another sentence, put brackets around your words to indicate the addition. If you omit something from a quotation, indicate the deletion with ellipsis marks, three periods preceded and followed by a space (. . .). (But generally avoid ellipses at the beginning or end of a quoted passage.) If you omit an entire line of verse from a quotation, indicate the omission with a line of periods stretching about the width of the verse. Adding or deleting words is permissible if necessary for clarity, as long as you don't alter the sense of the quoted passage, and as long as you flag the additions or deletions as described here.

APA

Quotations, like other material, are double-spaced and presented in the same font as body text.

Short quotations. For quotations of fewer than forty words, integrate the quotation into your body text and enclose it in quotation marks. If, as is usually the case, a parenthetical citation comes at the end of a sentence or clause, punctuation follows the citation (with the exception that question and exclamation marks if they are part of the quoted passage, should appear within the quotation marks):

> After this, Jan Kott says, Fortinbras "smiles and is very pleased with himself" (72).

Since short quotations from poetry (three or fewer lines) will be integrated into the body of your essay, mark the line breaks with a slash (/), preceded and followed by a space, between lines of verse. **Long (or block) quotations.** Quotes of forty or more words should be set off from the body text in a freestanding block. Quotation marks are not placed around the block quotation, which starts on a new line, indented one-half inch from the left margin. If you're citing a single paragraph, the first line is not indented; but if you're citing multiple paragraphs, each first line is indented an extra one-half inch. One important difference from short quotations: for block quotations the parenthetical citation comes after the closing punctuation mark. When quoting verse, maintain original line breaks and keep layout close to the original.

If you add words to a quotation, or alter a word to make the quoted passage fit grammatically in another sentence, put brackets around your words to indicate the addition (but you can change capitalization to fit your sentence without using brackets). If you omit something from a quotation, indicate the deletion with an ellipsis, three periods preceded and followed by a space (. . .)—or you may use your word-processing program's ellipsis character, preceded and followed by a space. If you are deleting a sentence break, signal that with four periods with spaces (or a period and your word processor's ellipsis character). Generally use ellipsis within quoted passages, not at the beginning or end of a quoted passage. If you omit an entire line of verse from a quotation, indicate the omission with a line of periods stretching about the width of the verse. Adding or deleting words is permissible if necessary for clarity, as long as you don't alter the sense of the quoted passage, and as long as you flag the additions or deletions as described here.

First-Page Formats

CMOS   Instructors may or may not require a separate title page. If required, the title should be centered about a third of the page from the top. It is usually in ALL CAPS, but some instructors may prefer Title Case. If you add a subtitle, put a colon after the title, then center the subtitle on a new line. After some white space, type your name, class information, and the submission date. If your title names a text, use the same formats as in the rest of your paper (italics for long works like books, quotation marks for short ones like stories and journal articles).

MLA   No separate title page. All header and title info is double-spaced (like the rest of the essay), with no extra blank lines. In the upper-left corner of the first page, list your name, instructor's name, course, and date, all double-spaced. Center the title but don't use special formatting (unless it includes quoted or emphasized words); write the title in Title Case, not ALL CAPS. If your title names a text, use the same formats as in the rest of your paper (italics for long works like books, quotation marks for short ones like stories and journal articles). Include the header on the first page.

APA   The first page is a separate title page. All matter on it is double-spaced. Pagination proceeds with the title page counting as the first page. The title should be centered vertically on the page, typed in the same font as the rest of the paper. It should not be bolded, underlined, or italicized. Write the title in Title Case, not ALL CAPS, and bold it. Capitalize major words. Below the title, also centered, put on separate centered lines your name, your affiliation (department and university), the course number and name, the instructor, and the date. For a visual example see the APA style blog: apastyle. apa.org/style-grammar-guidelines/paper-format/title-page.

      If your title names a text, use the same formats as in the rest of your paper (italics for long works like books, quotation marks for short ones like stories and journal articles). Any quoted title in your own title should be presented in Title Case, not ALL CAPS, with first words and subtitles, important words, and all words of four or more letters capitalized.

Abstract

Any instructor may require an abstract, a summary of the contents of a paper. It's a useful exercise because it forces the writer to distill the essence of her argument to a few words, being as clear as possible. Abstracts are common in the social sciences, so APA has a specific abstract format.

CMOS   If required, ask your instructor for guidance. Absent specific guidance, start the abstract on a separate page. At the top, center the word "Abstract," otherwise unformatted (including no quotation marks). Unless otherwise advised, aim for 150 to 200 words.

MLA If required, ask your instructor for guidance. Absent specific guidance, start the abstract on a separate page. At the top, center the word "Abstract," otherwise unformatted (including no quotation marks). Unless otherwise advised, aim for 150 to 250 words.

APA The abstract begins on a new page after the title page. It includes the page number. At the top, center the word "Abstract," otherwise unformatted (including no quotation marks). This line is double-spaced, but there is no extra white space or blank line added between the title and the body of the abstract. The abstract itself is a single paragraph of 150 to 250 words that summarizes the argument and key findings. The first line is not indented. Depending on the paper and the research method, it may be appropriate to include the research topic, questions, methods, results, analysis, and conclusions, and perhaps implications as well. You may also include keywords in the abstract. Do this by starting a new paragraph and indenting the first line. Type *Keywords*: (italicized) and then list the keywords (not italicized, lowercase, and separated by commas; no terminal period).

List of References

A list of references gathers together the sources you've used, with enough bibliographic information that the reader can retrace your steps. The list comes at the end of the paper, after any endnotes. The title of the list is centered at the top of a new page, continuing the paper's pagination. Entries are set off with a hanging indent: after the first line of each entry, subsequent lines are indented one-half inch (word processors automate this task). Don't skip lines between entries.

CMOS The usual title is "Bibliography," though other titles (e.g., "Works Cited" or "References") may be permitted. Below the title, insert two blank lines. It is common for teachers to prefer bibliographies to be single-spaced, with blank lines between entries, but CMOS does not specify this. The first line of each entry is flush left; additional lines are indented one-half inch. Capitalize all significant words in the titles of works listed. For additional details, see CMOS, chapter 14.

MLA   The usual title is "Works Cited." Capitalize all significant words in titles.

APA   The usual title is "References." Capitalize all major words in journal titles. For books and for the titles of journal articles, capitalize only the first word of each work's title, the first word after a colon, and names and acronyms. At the end of the reference, add a DOI (digital object identifier) or URL if available, in this format (note that there is no period after the DOI or URL): https://doi.org/10.1037/stl0000103

Basic Citation and Reference Formats

CMOS   In CMOS notes and bibliography style, when you cite a work you need a note (either footnote or endnote). This holds not only for direct quotes but also paraphrases and summaries. Adding notes is something word-processing programs handle easily; for each note, a superscript Arabic number in the text (at the end of the sentence or clause), will correspond to the same number at the start of the note, either at the bottom of the page or at the end of the section or whole document. The number that begins the note itself is in line with the rest of the note. The first line of the note is indented one-half inch, like a regular paragraph. Notes are double-spaced, with blank lines between them, unless your teacher specifies otherwise.

The first time you cite a source in a note, provide all required information, including author's name, title, publisher, and other details, depending on the source text. Subsequent citations of the source, anywhere in the paper, can leave out much of this, needing to include only the author's last name, a short version of the title (unless the original title is four or fewer words), and page number(s).

In a departure from previous CMOS usage, CMOS 17th edition prefers shortened citations for successive notes, rather than "ibid." See CMOS 14.34 for more details.

MLA   MLA is the most streamlined citation and reference style. Citations consist of the author's or authors' name(s), either integrated into your sentences or inserted as parentheticals. All other details are included in your works-cited list. Don't include titles (Dr., Prof.) with names, but do include Jr., etc.: "Mack, Maynard, Jr." For dates in references, MLA uses this format: 4 July 2012. Most months are abbreviated: Jan., Feb., Mar., Apr., May, June, July, Aug., Sept., Oct., Nov., Dec.

To locate and identify online sources, MLA prefers DOIs rather than URLs, as DOIs are more stable and thus more useful to others wishing to follow your citations. If you do use URLs, delete the initial "http://" element. MLA 8th edition no longer requires place or medium of publication.

MLA stresses the importance of identifying the "container" of a source—where the source is located. The container can be a book, a journal, a database, a website—any larger whole that the source is part of. Good MLA references are clear on both source and container.

APA APA citation style resembles MLA style, except year of publication is included with the name(s) of author(s). In-text citations may be parenthetical (all citation elements included in parentheses) or narrative (the author name[s] included in the text, and year and page references placed in a parenthetical). For references, italicize titles of journals and books. The new APA style (7th edition) no longer includes city of publication for books or book chapters. Do not italicize or otherwise specially format titles of articles or portions of larger works. Citing pages properly can be tricky, depending on what you cite. For in-text citations, identify all page numbers with "p." or, for multiple pages, "pp." But for items in the list of references, the formats vary. For matter from books and newspapers use "p." and "pp." But do not use these labels for identifying page numbers for articles from periodicals, including scholarly journals. When citing works by multiple authors, use "and" when naming the authors in the text of your essay, and the ampersand (&) when naming them in parentheticals and in the list of references.

Specific Citation and Reference Formats

1. An entire book
2. An entire article in a scholarly journal
3. Specific page(s), section(s), or chapter(s) cited from a book or article
4. Two authors
5. Three authors

1.   An entire book

CMOS   CITATION/NOTE: 1. First name Last name, *Title of Book* (Place of publication: Publisher, Year of publication).

1. Malcolm Gladwell, *The Tipping Point: How Little Things Can Make a Big Difference* (Boston: Back Bay Books, 2002).

REFERENCE: Last name, First name. *Title of Book.* Place of publication: Publisher, Year of publication.

Gladwell, Malcolm. *The Tipping Point: How Little Things Can Make a Big Difference.* Boston: Back Bay Books, 2002.

MLA   CITATION: Two main choices:

(1) (Gladwell).

(2) The author's name used in the body of the essay, so no parenthetical is needed.

REFERENCE: Last name, First name. *Title of Book.* Publisher, Year of publication.

Gladwell, Malcolm. *The Tipping Point: How Little Things Can Make a Big Difference.* Back Bay, 2002.

APA   **CITATION:** Two format choices, parenthetical (1) or narrative (2):

(l) (Gladwell, 2002).

(2) The author's name used in the body of the essay and the year of publication (and page references, if included) kept in parentheses, usually placed immediately after the name:

"Gladwell (2002) explores how a combination of small events can have large consequences."

REFERENCE: Last name, A. A. (Year of publication). *Title of book: Capital letter also for first word of subtitle.* Publisher.

Gladwell, M. (2002). *The tipping point: How little things can make a big difference.* Back Bay Books.

APA requires that the name of the publisher be given as concisely as possible: "Hackett" rather than "Hackett Publishing," and "Elgar" rather than "Edward Elgar"; but the words *Books* and *Press* should be retained, as in "Back Bay Books."

2. An entire article in a scholarly journal

CMOS   **CITATION/NOTE:** If the citation is to the whole article:

1. John S. Mebane, "'Impious War': Religion and the Ideology of Warfare in *Henry V*," *Studies in Philology* 104, no. 2 (Spring 2007).

2. Mebane, "'Impious War.'"

Note that in the short form of this title, only the quoted fragment is used to identify the title, so both the double quotation marks (here signifying an article title) and the single quotation marks (here signifying a quotation) are retained. The space between the single and double quotation marks is required, and to avoid peculiar line breaks it may be helpful to use a nonbreaking space in these instances.

REFERENCE: Mebane, John S. "'Impious War': Religion and the Ideology of Warfare in *Henry V.*" *Studies in Philology* 104, no. 2 (Spring 2007): 250–66.

If the article was accessed online, CMOS also requires inclusion of a URL or database information. See CMOS 14.175 for details, and items 32–34 below.

MLA   **CITATION:** (Mebane), or the author's name used in the body of the essay.

REFERENCE: Mebane, John S. "'Impious War': Religion and the Ideology of Warfare in *Henry V.*" *Studies in Philology*, vol. 104, no. 2, 2007, pp. 250–66.

APA

CITATION: Parenthetical: (Mebane, 2007). Narrative: "Mebane (2007) argues that. . . ." For specific pages in the in-text citation, use "p." for one page, and "pp." for multiple pages: (Mebane, 2007, p. 254). If the pages are discontinuous, use "pp." and place a comma between the page references: "pp. 253, 256."

REFERENCE: Last name, A. (Year). Title of article. *Title of Periodical, volume number* (issue number), pages. DOI

Wolin, S. (1982). America's civil religion. *Democracy: A Journal of Political Renewal and Radical Change, 2*(2), 7–17.

Note that there is no space between the italicized volume number and the unitalicized parenthesis. And note that for page references in the list of references, "p." or "pp." are not used.

3. Specific pages, section, or chapter(s) cited from a book or article

CMOS

CITATION/NOTE: l. Malcolm Gladwell, *The Tipping Point: How Little Things Can Make a Big Difference* (Boston: Back Bay Books, 2002), 32.

Brief form, for a subsequent citation: Gladwell, *Tipping Point*, 32.

REFERENCE: Even if you only cite one page in your essay, cite the largest unit the author is responsible for (the whole book, or a chapter in an edited book).

Gladwell, Malcolm. *The Tipping Point: How Little Things Can Make a Big Difference.* Boston: Back Bay Books, 2002.

MLA

CITATION: Two choices:

(1) (Gladwell 32).

(2) The author's name in a signal phrase, and the page number in parentheses:

Gladwell cites the famous ride of Paul Revere as an example of a "word-of-mouth epidemic" (32).

REFERENCE: Even if you only cite one page in your whole essay, cite the largest unit the author is responsible for (the whole book, or a chapter in an edited book).

>   Gladwell, Malcolm. *The Tipping Point: How Little Things Can Make a Big Difference.* Back Bay, 2002.

APA   **CITATION:** Three choices:
(1) Parenthetical: (Gladwell, 2002, p. 32).
(2) Narrative: The author's name in a signal phrase, and year of publication and page number in parentheses:

>   Gladwell cites the famous ride of Paul Revere as an example of a "word-of-mouth epidemic" (2002, p. 32).

(3) You may also place the parenthetical close to the author's name in the sentence:

>   Gladwell (2002, p. 32) cites the famous ride of Paul Revere as an example of a "word-of-mouth epidemic."

REFERENCE: Even if you only cite one page in your whole essay, cite the largest unit the author is responsible for (the whole book, or a chapter in an edited book).

>   Gladwell, M. (2002). *The tipping point: How little things can make a big difference.* Back Bay Books.

4. Two authors

CMOS   **CITATION/NOTE:** 1. Aaron Wildavsky and Karl Drake, "Theories of Risk Perception: Who Fears What and Why?" *Daedalus* 119, no. 4 (1990): 47.
2. Wildavsky and Drake, "Risk Perception," 52.
REFERENCE: Wildavsky, Aaron, and Karl Drake. "Theories of Risk Perception: Who Fears What and Why?" *Daedalus* 119, no. 4 (1990): 41–60.

MLA   **CITATION:** (Wildavsky and Drake 47).
REFERENCE: Wildavsky, Aaron, and Karl Drake. "Theories of Risk Perception: Who Fears What and Why?" *Daedalus*, vol. 119, no. 4, Fall 1990, pp. 41–60.

APA   **CITATION:** Parenthetical: (Wildavsky & Drake, 1990, p. 47).
Narrative: Wildavsky and Drake (1990, p. 47).
REFERENCE: Wildavsky, A., & Drake, K. (1990). Theories of risk perception: Who fears what and why? *Daedalus, 119*, 41–60.

5. Three authors

CMOS   **CITATION/NOTE:** Write out all last names.
REFERENCE: Only the first author's name is inverted.

MLA   **CITATION:** Write only the first author's last name, and replace the additional names with "et al." "Et al." is short for *et alii*, meaning "and others." The phrase is not italicized.
REFERENCE: Bligh, Michelle C., et al. "Charisma under Crisis: Presidential Leadership, Rhetoric, and Media Responses Before and After the September 11th Terrorist Attacks." *The Leadership Quarterly*, vol. 15, no. 2, April 2004, pp. 211–39.

APA   **CITATION:** Works with three or more authors use the first author's name followed by "et al." This is short for *et alii*, meaning "and others." The phrase is not italicized. Parenthetical: (Bligh et al., 2004). Narrative: Bligh et al. (2004) concluded that. . . .
REFERENCE: Bligh, M. C., Kohles, J. C., & Meindl, J. R. (2004). Charisma under crisis: Presidential leadership, rhetoric, and media responses before and after the September 11th terrorist attacks. *The Leadership Quarterly*, *15*(2), 211–239.

6. Four or five authors

CMOS   **CITATION/NOTE:** Write out the first author's name followed by "et al.," meaning "and others."
REFERENCE: Same as for three authors.

MLA   **CITATION:** Same as for three authors.
REFERENCE: Same as for three authors.

APA   **CITATION:** Same as for three authors.
REFERENCE: Same as for three authors.

7. Six or seven authors

CMOS   **CITATION/NOTE:** Same as for four authors.
REFERENCE: Same as for three authors.

MLA   **CITATION:** Same as for three authors.
REFERENCE: Same as for three authors.

APA   **CITATION:** Same as for three authors.
REFERENCE: Same as for three authors.

8. Eight to ten authors

CMOS   **CITATION/NOTE:** Same as for four authors.
            REFERENCE: Same as for three authors.

MLA   **CITATION:** Same as for three authors.
            REFERENCE: Same as for three authors.

APA   **CITATION:** Same as for three authors.
            REFERENCE: Same as for three authors.

9. Ten to twenty authors

CMOS   **CITATION/NOTE:** Same as for four authors.
            REFERENCE: List the first seven authors (with the first name inverted), followed by "et al."

MLA   **CITATION:** Same as for three authors.
            REFERENCE: Same as for three authors.

APA   **CITATION:** Same as for three authors.
            REFERENCE: Same as for three authors.
            (For more than twenty authors, list the first nineteen names, then an ellipsis, and then the last author.)

10. Corporate author or organization as author

CMOS   **CITATION/NOTE:** Treat the entity as the author.
            REFERENCE: Treat the entity as the author, alphabetizing by the first word (ignoring any initial article like "The").

MLA   **CITATION:** Treat the entity as the author, citing by a short version of the entity's name. If the author and publisher are the same entity, skip the author and alphabetize by title.
            REFERENCE: Treat the entity as the author, alphabetizing by the first word. Do not include "The" even if the organization uses it as the first word of its name.

APA   **CITATION:** Treat the entity as the author.
            REFERENCE: Treat the entity as the author, alphabetizing by the first word (ignoring any initial article like "The").

11. Anonymous or unlisted author

CMOS   **CITATION/NOTE:** The note begins with the title (ignoring the initial articles "A," "An," and "The").

REFERENCE: The reference begins with the title (including an initial article, but ignoring it for alphabetizing purposes).

MLA   **CITATION:** Cite the work in a signal phrase, and the page number in parentheses. Alternatively, cite the work and page number in parentheses.

REFERENCE: The reference begins with the title (including an initial "A," "An," or "The," but ignoring it for alphabetizing purposes).

APA   **CITATION:** Cite using a short version of the source's title, preserving formatting as appropriate. The reference begins with the title (including an initial article, but ignoring it for alphabetizing purposes).

(*Merriam-Webster's*, 2008).

REFERENCE: The reference begins with the title (including an initial article, but ignoring it for alphabetizing purposes).

Merriam-Webster's collegiate dictionary (11th ed.). (2008). Merriam-Webster.

12. Two or more works by same author

CMOS   **CITATION/NOTE:** No special rule.

REFERENCE: Within the overall list, alphabetized by author, order a given author's works alphabetically by title (ignoring the articles "A," "An," and "The"). For second and subsequent entries for the same author, repeat the author's name (note that this is new guidance for CMOS 17th edition, replacing previous guidance to use three em dashes instead of repeating names). Note that if a given author repeats, but as part of a team of authors that is different (or reversed), it is treated as a different author. Likewise, if a pair of authors co-author multiple works, but switch the published order of their names, treat these as different authors; in each instance alphabetize by the last name of the first author.

MLA   **CITATION:** In addition to the author's name, use a short form of the title to specify which work is being cited, using italics for books and quotation marks for articles. If the author appears in your sentence, then the parenthetical need only include the short title and page number (with no comma).

Weber argued against this interpretation (*Economy and Society* 217).

REFERENCE: Within the overall list, alphabetized by author, order a given author's works alphabetically by title (ignoring "A," "An," and "The"). For second and subsequent entries for the same author, use three hyphens and a period instead of the author's name. Note that if a given author repeats, but as part of a team of authors that is different (or reversed), then that is treated as a different author. Likewise, if a pair of authors co-author multiple works, but switch the order of their names, treat these as different authors; in each instance alphabetize by the last name of the first author.

APA   **CITATION:** (Lowi, 1964, 1968).
REFERENCE: Use the author's name, and list by year, with earliest first.

Lowi, T. J. (1964).

Lowi, T. J. (1968).

If the author appears in your list as a single author and in a separate citation as the first author of a collaboration, list any single-author texts first.

13. Two or more works by same author in same year

CMOS   **CITATION/NOTE:** No special rule.
REFERENCE: No special rule.

MLA   **CITATION:** Same as for two or more works by the same author.
REFERENCE: Same as for two or more works by the same author.

APA   **CITATION:** (Smith, 2007a).
(Smith, 2007b).

REFERENCE: List alphabetically by title, then add letter suffixes (a, b, etc.) to the year.

14. Single-author book with editor

CMOS   **CITATION/NOTE:** Henry David Thoreau, *Collected Poems*, ed. Carl Bode (Baltimore: Johns Hopkins University Press, 1965).
REFERENCE: Thoreau, Henry David. *Collected Poems*. Edited by Carl Bode. Baltimore: Johns Hopkins University Press, 1965.

MLA   **CITATION:** No special rule.
            REFERENCE: Thoreau, Henry David. *Collected Poems*. Edited
            by Carl Bode, Johns Hopkins UP, 1965.

APA   **CITATION:** No special rule.
            REFERENCE: Thoreau, H. D. (1965). *Collected Poems* (C. Bode,
            Ed.). Johns Hopkins University Press.

15.   Book previously published

CMOS   **CITATION/NOTE:** No special rule. Including the original date
            of publication is permissible but not required.
            REFERENCE: No special rule.

MLA   **CITATION:** No special rule.
            REFERENCE: Smith, Adam. *Wealth of Nations*. 1776. Bantam,
            2003.

APA   **CITATION:** (Smith, 1776/2003).
            REFERENCE: Smith, A. (2003). *Wealth of Nations* (A. B. Krueger,
            Ed.). Bantam Books. (Original work published 1776.)

16.   Item from a collection of the author's work

CMOS   **CITATION/NOTE:** 1. Ha Jin, "A Report" in *Ocean of Words:
            Army Stories* (Cambridge, MA: Zoland Books, 1996), 1–4.
            If a specific page is being cited, cite only that page in the note.
            REFERENCE: Jin, Ha. "A Report." In *Ocean of Words: Army
            Stories*, 1–4. Cambridge, MA: Zoland Books, 1996.

MLA   **CITATION:** No special rule.
            REFERENCE: Jin, Ha. "A Report." *Ocean of Words: Army Stories*,
            Zoland, 1996, pp. 1–4.

APA   **CITATION:** No special rule.
            REFERENCE: Jin, H. (1996). A report. In H. Jin, *Ocean of words:
            Army stories* (pp. 1–4). Zoland Books.

17.   Edited book

CMOS   **CITATION/NOTE:** 1. Michael Harvey and Ronald E. Riggio, eds.,
            Leadership Studies: The Dialogue of Disciplines (Northampton,
            MA: Edward Elgar, 2011).

REFERENCE: Harvey, Michael, and Ronald E. Riggio, eds. *Leadership Studies: The Dialogue of Disciplines.* Northampton, MA: Edward Elgar, 2011.

MLA   **CITATION:** No special rule.
REFERENCE: Harvey, Michael, and Ronald E. Riggio, editors. *Leadership Studies: The Dialogue of Disciplines.* Elgar, 2011.

APA   **CITATION:** No special rule.
REFERENCE: Harvey, M., & Riggio, R. E. (Eds.). (2011). *Leadership studies: The dialogue of disciplines.* Elgar.

18. Chapter from an edited book

CMOS   **CITATION/NOTE:** 1. Stephen P. Turner, "Classic Sociology: Weber as an Analyst of Charisma," in *Leadership Studies: The Dialogue of Disciplines,* ed. Michael Harvey and Ronald E. Riggio (Northampton, MA: Edward Elgar, 2011), 85.
REFERENCE: Turner, Stephen P. "Classic Sociology: Weber as an Analyst of Charisma." In *Leadership Studies: The Dialogue of Disciplines,* edited by Michael Harvey and Ronald E. Riggio, 82–88. Northampton, MA: Edward Elgar, 2011.

MLA   **CITATION:** No special rule.
REFERENCE: Turner, Stephen P. "Classic Sociology: Weber as an Analyst of Charisma." *Leadership Studies: The Dialogue of Disciplines,* edited by Michael Harvey and Ronald E. Riggio, Elgar, 2011, pp. 82–88.

APA   **CITATION:** No special rule.
REFERENCE: Turner, S. P. (2011). Classic sociology: Weber as an analyst of charisma. In M. Harvey & R. E. Riggio (Eds.), *Leadership studies: The dialogue of disciplines* (pp. 82–88). Elgar.

19. Citations of multiple chapters from a multi-author anthology

CMOS   **CITATION/NOTE:** Once an anthology has been cited, subsequent citations can cite the anthology by editor(s) and short title (see CMOS 14.108).
REFERENCE: Turner, Stephen P. "Classic Sociology: Weber as an Analyst of Charisma." In Harvey and Riggio, *Leadership Studies,* 82–88. The anthology would also be included in the bibliography.

MLA   CITATION: No special rule.

REFERENCE: If you cite several works by different authors from one collection, you may wish to cross-reference your works to reduce the amount of copied information in your list of works cited.

Here's how: First, create a regular reference entry for the edited collection, following the normal format for such a work. Then, for each individual work cited from this collection, you may use an abbreviated reference:

> Turner, Stephen P. "Classic Sociology: Weber as an Analyst of Charisma." Harvey and Riggio, pp. 82–88.

APA   CITATION: No special rule.
REFERENCE: No special rule.

20.   Preface, foreword, introduction, afterword, etc.

CMOS   CITATION/NOTE: 1. John O'Meara, introduction to *Concerning the City of God Against the Pagans*, by Augustine (Harmondsworth, UK: Penguin, 1972), vii–xxxv.

2. O'Meara, introduction, xxxvii.

REFERENCE: O'Meara, John. Introduction to *Concerning the City of God Against the Pagans*, by Augustine, vii–xxxv. Harmondsworth, UK: Penguin, 1972.

MLA   CITATION: No special rule.
REFERENCE: O'Meara, John. Introduction. *Concerning the City of God Against the Pagans*, by Augustine, Penguin, 1972, pp. vii–xxxv.

APA   CITATION: No special rule.
REFERENCE: Cite as usual, with the appropriate term (Foreword, Introduction, etc.) in place of a chapter title.

21.   Works by authors with the same last name

CMOS   CITATION/NOTE: No special rule.

MLA   CITATION: Include first initials in the citations (or full first names, if needed to avoid confusion).

APA   CITATION: Include first and middle initials in the citation. (R. S. Jenkins, 2011).

22. Author with translator

CMOS **CITATION/NOTE:** 1. Galileo Galilei, *Dialogue Concerning the Two Chief World Systems—Ptolemaic and Copernican*, trans. Stillman Drake (Berkeley and Los Angeles: University of California Press, 1953).
REFERENCE: Galilei, Galileo. *Dialogue Concerning the Two Chief World Systems—Ptolemaic and Copernican*. Translated by Stillman Drake. Berkeley and Los Angeles: University of California Press, 1953.

MLA **CITATION:** No special rule.
REFERENCE: Galilei, Galileo. *Dialogue Concerning the Two Chief World Systems—Ptolemaic and Copernican*. Translated by Stillman Drake, U of California P, 1953.

APA **CITATION:** No special rule.
REFERENCE: Galilei, G. (1953). *Dialogue concerning the two chief world systems—Ptolemaic and Copernican* (S. Drake, Trans.). University of California Press.

23. Second or subsequent edition

CMOS **CITATION/NOTE:** 1. Michael Harvey, *The Nuts and Bolts of College Writing*, 3rd ed. (Indianapolis: Hackett, 2020), 55.
REFERENCE: Harvey, Michael. *The Nuts and Bolts of College Writing*. 3rd ed. Indianapolis: Hackett, 2020.

MLA **CITATION:** No special rule.
REFERENCE: Harvey, Michael. *The Nuts and Bolts of College Writing*. 3rd ed., Hackett, 2020.

APA **CITATION:** No special rule.
REFERENCE: Harvey, M. (2020). *The nuts and bolts of college writing* (3rd ed.). Hackett.

24. Multivolume work

CMOS **CITATION/NOTE:** Specify the volume and page number being cited:

> Winston S. Churchill, *The Second World War* (Boston: Houghton Mifflin, 1948–53), 6:269.

Or, if the entire volume is being cited in the note:

Winston S. Churchill, *The Second World War* (Boston: Houghton Mifflin, 1948–53), vol. 6.

REFERENCE: Churchill, Winston S. *The Second World War.* 6 vols. Boston: Houghton Mifflin, 1948–53.

MLA   CITATION: Specify the volume being cited.

(Churchill 6: 269).

REFERENCE: Churchill, Winston S. *The Second World War.* Houghton Mifflin, 1948–53. 6 vols.

APA   CITATION: Make sure that the date used matches that in the reference list. If pagination resets with each volume, you should specify the volume along with the page reference.

(Churchill, 1948–1953, vol. 6, p. 269).

REFERENCE: Churchill, W. S. (1948–1953). *The second world war* (Vols. 1–6). Houghton Mifflin.

25. One volume from a multivolume work

CMOS   CITATION/NOTE: Match the citation to the form chosen for the reference (see below).

1. Winston S. Churchill, *The Second World War*, vol. 6, *Triumph and Tragedy* (Boston: Houghton Mifflin, 1953), 269.

or

1. Winston S. Churchill, *Triumph and Tragedy*, vol. 6 of *The Second World War* (Boston: Houghton Mifflin, 1953), 269.

REFERENCE: Churchill, Winston S. *The Second World War.* Vol. 6, *Triumph and Tragedy*. Boston: Houghton Mifflin, 1953.

or

Churchill, Winston S. *Triumph and Tragedy*. Vol. 6 of *The Second World War*. Boston: Houghton Mifflin, 1953.

MLA   CITATION: If you cite only one volume from a multivolume work you don't need to specify the volume in your in-text citation: (Churchill 269), or just the page reference (269) if the author appears in a signal phrase in your text.

REFERENCE: The reference specifies the volume: Churchill, Winston S. *The Second World War*. Vol. 6, Houghton Mifflin, 1953.

APA **CITATION:** No special rule.
    REFERENCE: Churchill, W. S. (1948–1953). *The second world war* (Vol. 6). Houghton Mifflin.

26. Print dictionary or encyclopedia, unsigned article

CMOS **CITATION/NOTE:** 1. *Oxford English Dictionary*, 2nd ed., s.v. "window."
    The abbreviation s.v. (not italicized) for *sub verbo*, "under the word," is used to signify entries in dictionaries and encyclopedias.
    By convention, citation of widely used reference works like the OED include edition but not year of publication.
    REFERENCE: Not usually included in the bibliography.

MLA **CITATION:** Cite by the defined word or term. If the reference is organized alphabetically, do not include page information. If you are citing a dictionary for other purposes, identify the editor or author and treat it as any other book, or cite the pertinent portion of the book, such as the foreword.
    REFERENCE: "Window." *Oxford English Dictionary*, 2nd ed., 1989.
    For standard reference works like the *OED* or the *Encyclopedia Britannica*, don't provide full publishing information, just the year of publication. For specialized reference works, treat the referenced article as a chapter from an edited book.

APA APA style (7th edition) no longer gives specific guidance on physical reference books, encouraging students to cite electronic reference works (see below for guidance). If you do cite a physical reference work, follow APA guidelines for books, or articles from books (see above).

27. Print dictionary or reference work, signed article

CMOS **CITATION/NOTE:** Treat as a chapter in a book.
    REFERENCE: Treat as a chapter in a book.

MLA **CITATION:** Cite by author; follow format for chapter from a book.
    REFERENCE: No special rule.

APA APA style (7th edition) no longer gives specific guidance on physical reference books, encouraging students to cite electronic reference works (see below for guidance). If you do cite a physical reference work, follow APA guidelines for books, or articles from books (see above).

28. Print newspaper article

CMOS **CITATION/NOTE:** Newspapers (including articles, editorials, letters to the editor, etc.) are commonly only cited in notes (or parenthetical references, even when using CMOS notes and bibliography style). They are not commonly included in the bibliography. Page numbers are usually omitted for newspapers.

Adam Bryant, "Distilling the Wisdom of C.E.O.'s," *New York Times*, April 16, 2011.

Or, as an in-text parenthetical reference:

After interviewing more than 70 business leaders, journalist Adam Bryant suggests that good CEOs possess "passionate curiosity" ("Distilling the Wisdom of C.E.O.'s," *New York Times*, April 16, 2011).

REFERENCE: A reference, if desired, can be included. Page numbers are usually not included, but URLs are.
Print source:

Bryant, Adam. "Distilling the Wisdom of C.E.O.'s." *New York Times*, April 16, 2011. New York edition.

Online source:

Bryant, Adam. "Distilling the Wisdom of C.E.O.'s." *New York Times*, April 16, 2011, http://www.nytimes.com/2011/04/17/business/17excerpt.html.

MLA **CITATION:** No special rule.
REFERENCE: Bryant, Adam. "Distilling the Wisdom of C.E.O.'s." *New York Times*, New York ed., 16 Apr. 2011, p. BU1.

APA **CITATION:** No special rule.
REFERENCE: Bryant, A. (2011, April 16). Distilling the wisdom of C.E.O.'s. *New York Times*, p. BU1.

29. Print unsigned editorial

CMOS **CITATION/NOTE:** 1. Editorial, *New York Times*, April 30, 2012.
REFERENCE: Not usually included in the bibliography. If you wish to include, use name of publication as the author.

To cite an editorial accessed online, include a URL or DOI (see below for details).

MLA   CITATION: No special rule.
REFERENCE: "Bigotry on the Ballot." Editorial. *New York Times*, Washington ed., 30 Apr. 2012, p. A22.

APA   CITATION: ("Bigotry on the Ballot," 2012).
REFERENCE: Bigotry on the ballot [Editorial]. (2012, April 30). *New York Times*, p. A22.

30. Review of book, film, performance, etc.

CMOS CITATION/NOTE: Provide these elements in the following order: 1. reviewer name, if provided; review title; the words "review of" followed by the name of the work reviewed and its author/creator; location and date of performance, if applicable; the periodical or publication information; URL or DOI, if online source.

1. Anthony Tommasini, review of *Der Ring des Nibelungen*, by Richard Wagner, directed by Robert Lepage, Metropolitan Opera, New York, *New York Times*, April 26, 2012, https:// www.nytimes.com/2012/04/26/arts/music/robert-lepages -first-complete-ring-concludes-at-met.html.

REFERENCE: Not usually included in the bibliography.

MLA   CITATION: No special rule.
REFERENCE: Tommasini, Anthony. "Met's 'Ring' Machine Finishes the Spin Cycle." Review of *Der Ring des Nibelungen*, by Richard Wagner. *New York Times*, 26 Apr. 2012, www.nytimes.com /2012/04/26/arts/music/robert-lepages-first-complete-ring-con cludes-at-met.html.

APA   CITATION: No special rule.
REFERENCE: Tommasini, A. (2012, April 26). Met's "Ring" machine finishes the spin cycle. [Review of Der Ring des Nibelungen, by R. Wagner.] *New York Times*, p. Cl.

31. Print letter to the editor

CMOS CITATION/NOTE: 1. William H. Barnwell, letter to the editor, *New York Times*, April 30, 2012.
REFERENCE: Not usually included in the bibliography.

MLA   **CITATION:** No special rule.
              REFERENCE: Barnwell, William H. Letter. *New York Times*,
              Washington ed., 30 Apr. 2012, p. A22.

APA   **CITATION:** No special rule.
              REFERENCE: Barnwell, W. H. (2012, April 30). Bring back
              learning for learning's sake. [Letter to the editor.] *New York Times*,
              p. A22.

32.   General format for online and electronic sources: DOIs and URLs

Besides the familiar URL, many online sources, especially scholarly texts, include a special digital object identifier (DOI). Journal articles in a database, for
instance, often include a DOI.

CMOS   **CITATION/NOTE:** Notes citing online sources should include a
              URL or, preferably, a DOI.
              REFERENCE: When available, cite author, title, description, and
              website.
                  As the final element of an online citation, include either a DOI
              or a URL. (For material accessed via other electronic formats, for
              instance a CD-ROM, the medium should be indicated.) Provide a
              date of publication or revision; if this is not available, provide an
              access date, with the word "accessed" before the date.
                  CMOS recommends using short forms for URLs when possible,
              and suggests exploring navigation tools to find better (shorter)
              URLs. When a short URL is not available, CMOS permits the use
              of the domain name or the name of the database in which the source
              was found rather than a specific URL to the source. But CMOS
              cautions against using short versions of URLs provided by
              link-shortening third parties. For more details, see CMOS 14.10.

MLA   **CITATION:** No special rule.
              REFERENCE: MLA 8th edition requires DOIs (preferred) or
              URLs in references to online sources, and encourages the use of
              citing containers (the names of databases or websites from which
              you accessed specific sources. For URL format, don't include the
              http:// portion of the locator. If an online source has a permanent
              link (a "permalink"), use it as the URL. If, as is often the case with
              online texts, there are no page numbers, you may instead refer to
              paragraph numbers ("par." for a single paragraph, "pars." for mul-
              tiple). Generally, MLA format for online sources should include

author, source (article or equivalent in quotation marks, book or equivalent in italics), container title (this would be the website or database or the like), version (including edition, revision, issue number), publisher information, page or paragraph information, DOI or URL, and, if no other date is provided, the date you accessed the source, beginning with "Accessed."

APA   For APA 7th edition, a DOI must now include the entire URL, not simply begin with "doi." In other words APA no longer distinguishes DOIs and URLs as different kinds of identifiers. URLs are no longer preceded by "Retrieved from."

CITATION: No special rule.

REFERENCE: All online sources must include either a URL, a DOI, or other locator.

DOI format

Last name, A. A. (Year). Title of document. http://doi:xxxxxxxxxx

> Lisk, T. C., Kaplancali, U. T., & Riggio, R. E. (2012, March). Leadership in multiplayer online gaming environments. *Simulation & Gaming, 43*(1), 133–149. http://doi:10 .1177/1046878110391975

Note that "doi" is not capitalized, the colon has no space after it, and there is no final period.

URL format

> Last name, A. A. (Year). Title of document. http://URL

If a more precise date would be helpful, use the date format (year, month day). Do not underline or place a period after the URL. If the format is unusual, like a blog post or lecture notes, then include a format description in brackets:

> Last name, A. A. (Year). Title of document [Format description, like online forum post or tweet]. http://URL

33.   Journal article accessed via proprietary database

CMOS   **CITATION/NOTE:** Use a DOI if available. If not, a URL may not be very useful for gated databases requiring login—CMOS recommends providing the name of the database instead.

1. Victoria L. Brescoll and Eric Luis Uhlmann, "Can an Angry Woman Get Ahead?" *Psychological Science* 19, no. 3 (2008): 271, Academic Search Premier, doi:10.1111/j.1467 -9280.2008.02079.x.

REFERENCE: Brescoll, Victoria L., and Eric Luis Uhlmann. "Can an Angry Woman Get Ahead?" *Psychological Science* 19, no. 3 (2008): 268–75. Academic Search Premier, doi:10.1111/j .1467-9280.2008.02079.x.

MLA CITATION: No special rule.
REFERENCE: Stanton, Kay. "Intersections of Politics, Culture, Class, and Gender in Shakespeare's *Titus Andronicus*, *The Taming of the Shrew*, and *The Merchant of Venice*." *Multicultural Shakespeare*, vol. 12, no. 27 (2015), pp. 41–54. ProQuest, doi:10.1515/mstap -2015-0004.

APA CITATION: No special rule.
REFERENCE: Brescoll, V. L., & Uhlmann, E. L. (2008). Can an angry woman get ahead? *Psychological Science*, *19*(3), 268–275. https://doi:10.1111/j.1467-9280.2008.02079.x

34. Journal article in online-only journal

CMOS CITATION/NOTE: Treat as a regular journal article, appending a DOI if available, and a URL if not.
REFERENCE: Treat as a regular journal article, appending a DOI if available, and a URL if not.

MLA CITATION: No special rule, except that online publications often lack page numbers. You may count by paragraphs, using the abbreviation "par." or "pars." (for paragraph or paragraphs).
REFERENCE: Same as a print publication. Provide a DOI or URL.

APA CITATION: No special rule.
REFERENCE: Follow the example for a journal accessed via a proprietary database.

35. E-book

CMOS REFERENCE: Isaacson, Walter. *Steve Jobs*. New York: Simon & Schuster, 2011. Kindle.

Many e-books are based on prior print editions. Including information about the prior edition is optional. E-books sometimes lack stable page numbers; in such cases, include chapter, section, or other locator. For more details see CMOS 14.159.

MLA   REFERENCE: Isaacson, Walter. *Steve Jobs*. Kindle ed., Simon & Schuster, 2011.

APA   REFERENCE: Same as for a print book, but include the DOI if available.

Last name, A. A. (Year). *Title of book*. Publisher. http:// doi:xxxxx

If the book was read via an academic database and has no DOI, the reference follows the same format as for a print book—it ends after the publisher, and does not mention the database.

36. Entire website

CMOS   CITATION/NOTE: Shakespeare Globe Trust. Shakespeare's Globe, 2012. https://www.shakespearesglobe.com/.
If no publication or revision date is available, include an access date preceded by "accessed." Include "website" after title if it clarifies the source. For more details see CMOS 14.207.
REFERENCE: Not usually included in the bibliography.

MLA   CITATION: No special rule.
REFERENCE: Olsen, Corey. *The Tolkien Professor*. Mythgard Institute, www.tolkienprofessor.com. Accessed 22 Sept. 2018.

APA   Do not cite or provide a reference for whole websites. If you do wish to mention a website, do so in the text and include the URL in parentheses.

37. Blog post and blog, with author

CMOS   CITATION/NOTE: 1. Mickey Kaus, "Volt Is to Dog Food. . . ." *KausFiles* (blog), *The Daily Caller*, April 29, 2012, https://daily caller.com/2012/04/29/why-the-volts-flopping/.
REFERENCE: Not included in the bibliography.

MLA   CITATION: No special rule.
REFERENCE: McDonough, Megan. "Is the Internet Killing Language? LOL, No." *Vox*, 29 July 2019, www.vox.com/the-highlight

/2019/7/22/20702335/internet-language-text-emojis-gifs-bad
-for-english.

APA   CITATION: No special rule.
            REFERENCE: Kaus, M. (2012, April 29). Volt is to dog food. . . .
            Daily Caller https://dailycaller.com/2012/04/29/why-the-volts
            -flopping/

38.   Website post or page, no author (blogs, etc.)

CMOS   CITATION/NOTE: Include the title or page description; title of
            site as a whole; owner or sponsor of site; publication or revision
            date; and URL OR DOI. You may add the word "web page" in
            parentheses after the title or description if helpful. See CMOS
            14.207 for more details.

            1. "The Dish Awards," *The Dish* (blog), *The Daily Beast*,
            April 4, 2011, http://dish.andrewsullivan.com/2011/12/30/
            the-2011-dish-awards-the-winners/.

            REFERENCE: Not included in the bibliography.

MLA   CITATION: Cite by title.
            REFERENCE: Alphabetize by title.

APA   CITATION: (Dish Awards, 2011).
            REFERENCE: Include a format description in brackets after the
            title of the document. (When there is no author the title will come
            first, then date, then format description.)

            The dish awards. (2011, May 30). *Daily Caller.* Retrieved
            from http://andrewsullivan.thedailybeast.com/awards.html.
            Note that this would alphabetized in the reference list under
            "D."

39.   Online dictionary or encyclopedia

CMOS   CITATION/NOTE: Cite like a print reference work, adding a
            posted publication date if available, or access date if note. As the
            last citation element include a URL or DOI, use the entry's recom-
            mended form, if provided.
            REFERENCE: Not usually included in the bibliography. For some
            specialized dictionaries or encyclopedias with "substantial, au-
            thored entries" (CMOS 14.234), it may be appropriate to cite indi-
            vidual entries, and include them in the bibliography.

MLA   **CITATION:** No special rule.
           REFERENCE: No special rule. Follow the usual format for refer-
           ences, and include a DOI or URL.

APA   **CITATION:** No special rule.
           REFERENCE: Entries in online dictionaries can change, so in
           this instance include "Retrieved from" and a date.

> Merriam-Webster. (n.d.). Heuristic. In *Merriam-Webster's
> online dictionary* (11th ed.). Retrieved December 17, 2019,
> from https://www.merriam-webster.com/dictionary/heuristic

40. Wikipedia

CMOS   **CITATION/NOTE:** 1. Wikipedia, s.v. "2019-nCoV acute respira-
           tory disease," last modified February 14, 2020, https://en.wikipe-
           dia.org/wiki/2019nCoV_acute_respiratory_disease.
               The abbreviation s.v. (not italicized) for *sub verbo,* "under the
           word," is used to signify entries in dictionaries and ency-
           clopedias.
           REFERENCE: Not usually included in the bibliography.

MLA   **CITATION:** No special rule.
           REFERENCE: "2019-nCoV acute respiratory disease." *Wikipe-
           dia: The Free Encyclopedia,*

> Wikimedia Foundation, 14 Feb. 2020, https://en.wikipedia
> .org/wiki/2019nCoV_acute_respiratory_disease.

APA   **CITATION:** No special rule.
           REFERENCE: Since the content is unstable, your date of retrieval
           should be included.

> 2019-nCoV acute respiratory disease. (2020, February 14).
> In *Wikipedia.* https://en.wikipedia.org/wiki/2019nCoV_acute
> _respiratory_disease

41. Social media content

CMOS   **CITATION/NOTE:** Cite publicly available social media content
           (not private messages—see CMOS 14.214) by including the follow-
           ing elements:
           • Author (real name, if known, followed by a screen name in
             parentheses—omit the parentheses if the real name is not
             known).

- In lieu of title, the actual text of the post, up to the first 160 spaces, including spaces, capitalized as in the original (but if the post has been quoted in your text, do not repeat it in the note).
- Type of post, including name of social media service and description of the type of post, if relevant.
- Date.
- URL.

REFERENCE: Not included in the bibliography. See CMOS 14.209 for more details.

MLA   CITATION: As much as possible, handle social media content like other sources, by providing author, title, source, and date.

For a tweet, treat the user's Twitter handle as the name. Place the entire tweet in quotations, ending with a period and followed by URL. Provide the post's date and time, separated with a comma. You may include date accessed. For other kinds of social media content, see specific guidance at the MLA Style Center website, style.mla.org/styling-online-works/.

APA   CITATION: No special rule.
REFERENCE: Bleacher Report [@BleacherReport]. (2020, February 13). *Astros players apologize for the cheating scandal* [Tweet]. Twitter. https://twitter.com/BleacherReport/status /1227966047824883715

42. Email

CMOS   CITATION/NOTE: 1. Donald McColl, email message to author, March 12, 2012.

If the description and date are integrated into the body of the essay, no note is needed.
REFERENCE: Not included in the bibliography.

MLA   CITATION: No special rule.
REFERENCE: McColl, Donald. "Re: Leadership and Art." Received by Michael Harvey, 12 March 2012.

APA   CITATION: D. A. McColl (personal communication, March 12, 2012), or (D. A. McColl, personal communication, March 12, 2012).
REFERENCE: Not included in the reference list.

43. YouTube video or similar source

CMOS   **CITATION/NOTE:** Include information about author or per-
            former, title, series or source, date, type of multimedia, and length.
            See CMOS 14.267 for more details.

                1. Jennifer Finney Boylan, "A Transgender Path Home,"
                TEDxMet, Sept. 30, 2015, video, 10:11, https://www.you-
                tube.com/watch?v=I0h7LFvlVwk.

            REFERENCE: Not included in the bibliography

MLA   **CITATION:** No special rule.
            REFERENCE: No special rule. Make sure to include a DOI or
            URL.

APA   **CITATION:** (TEDxMet, 2015).
            REFERENCE: TEDxMet. (2015, September 30). *A transgender
            path home* [Video]. YouTube. https://www.youtube.com/watch
            ?v=I0h7LFvlVwk

                In cases like this, where an organization uploaded a video of a
            talk by an individual, but you wish to discuss the individual, ex-
            plain this in the text.

44. Film

CMOS   **CITATION/NOTE:** 1. *Apocalypse Now*, directed by Francis Ford
            Coppola (1979; Hollywood, CA: Paramount, 2001), DVD.
                Note that the original release date and the DVD release date are
            both included.
            REFERENCE: *Apocalypse Now*. Directed by Francis Ford Cop-
            pola. Hollywood, CA: Paramount, 1979. DVD.
                See CMOS 14.267–68 for additional details.

MLA   **CITATION:** Match the reference format, either by title (as in the
            example below), or by director.
            REFERENCE: *Apocalypse Now*. Directed by Francis Ford Cop-
            pola, Paramount, 1979.

APA   **CITATION:** No special rule.
            REFERENCE: Coppola, F. F. (Director). (1979). *Apocalypse now*
            [Film]. Paramount.

45. Published dissertation or thesis

CMOS **CITATION/NOTE:** Treat like a book, except that the title appears in quotation marks, not italics. After the title, note the kind of thesis, academic institution, and date—in parentheses in the note. If the dissertation was accessed online, include a URL or the name of the database and, in parentheses, any identification number. If the dissertation was accessed via microfiche or microfilm, note this as well at the end of the note (see CMOS 14.115 for more details).
REFERENCE: Treat like a book, except that the title appears in quotation marks rather than italics—in this and other details, follow the citation guidelines above.

> Venkatesh, Sudhir Alladi. "American Project: An Historical-Ethnography of Chicago's Robert Taylor Homes." Doctoral Dissertation. University of Chicago. 1997. Dissertation Abstracts International. Database: America: History & Life (45885433).

MLA **CITATION:** No special rule.
REFERENCE: Italicize the title. Add "PhD dissertation" (or "MA dissertation" or other appropriate designation) after the title. Include the publication date. Including the degree-granting institution is optional.

> Stephen Hawking. *Properties of Expanding Universes.* 1966. University of Cambridge, PhD dissertation. doi.org/10 .17863/CAM.11283.

APA **CITATION:** No special rule.
REFERENCE: Specify the type of dissertation.
Last name, A. (Year). *Title of dissertation* (Accession or Order Number) [Doctoral dissertation, Name of University]. Name of database.

> Venkatesh, S. A. (1997). *American project: An historical-ethnography of Chicago's Robert Taylor Homes* [Doctoral dissertation, University of Chicago]. Dissertation Abstracts International.

46. Unpublished personal interview

CMOS   **CITATION/NOTE:** If the interviewee consents to have his or her name used, note as follows:

> Joseph Matthews (student-athlete), interview with the author, March 14, 2012.

If a transcript or recording is available, note where it may be found.

If the interviewee wishes not to be identified, or if your judgment is that using the name might be imprudent or dangerous, the first such note should explain the absence of the name, in language similar to this:

> 1. Interview with student-athlete, March 14, 2012. Name of interviewee withheld.

REFERENCE: Unpublished interviews do not usually appear in the bibliography.

MLA   **CITATION:** If the interviewee has given consent to being identified and having the interview published or referenced, he or she may be cited by name. In the citation, the interviewee is treated as the author. If such consent has not been given, obscure the identity of the interviewee with an identification of role, an alias, or by letter.

REFERENCE: Adhere to the consent and identification guidelines as for the citation. You may specify the type of interview.

> Ojubwe, Madeo. Oral interview. 23 Mar. 2019.

> Atkinson, Steven. Email interview. 7 June 2019.

APA   **CITATION:** If the interviewee has given consent to being identified and having the interview published or referenced, follow this format:

> J. Matthews (personal communication, March 14, 2012), or
> (J. Matthews, personal communication, March 14, 2012).

If such consent has not been given, obscure the identity of the interviewee with an identification of role, an alias, or by letter:

> (Interviewee B, March 14, 2012).

> (Student-athlete, March 14, 2012).

REFERENCE: Not included in reference list.

47. Published interview

CMOS   **CITATION/NOTE:** Treat like an article in a periodical. Interviews accessed online should include a URL.
REFERENCE: Watterson, Bill. "Bill Watterson Creator of Beloved 'Calvin and Hobbes' Comic Strip, Looks Back with No Regrets." By John Campanelli. *Cleveland Plain Dealer*, February 1, 2010.

MLA   **CITATION:** Treat like an article in a periodical or chapter in a book, with the interview subject as author.
REFERENCE: If the interview is contained in another work, you may include the interviewer's name:

> Watterson, Bill. "Bill Watterson, Creator of Beloved 'Calvin and Hobbes' Comic Strip, Looks Back with No Regrets." Interview conducted by John Campanelli. *Cleveland Plain Dealer*, 1 Feb. 2010, www.cleveland.com/living/2010/02 /bill_watterson_creator_of_belo.html.

APA   **CITATION:** Treat like an article in a periodical or chapter in a book: (author, date).
REFERENCE: Campanelli, J. (2010, February 1). Bill Watterson, creator of beloved "Calvin and Hobbes" comic strip, looks back with no regrets. *Cleveland Plain Dealer*. https://www.cleveland .com/living/2010/02/bill_watterson_creator_of_belo.html

48. Book published before 1900

CMOS   **CITATION/NOTE:** For books published before 1900, the publisher's name may be omitted.

> Nahum Tate, *The History of King Lear* (London, 1745).

REFERENCE: Tate, Nahum. *The History of King Lear*. London, 1745.

MLA   **CITATION:** No special rule.
REFERENCE: You may omit the publisher and, in an exception for MLA 8th edition, include place of publication: Tate, Nahum. *The History of King Lear*, London, 1745.

APA   **CITATION:** No special rule.
REFERENCE: No special rule.

49. Classical and classic texts

CMOS   **CITATION/NOTE:** Classical works usually have conventional textual division numbers for books, sections, lines, and the like. Page numbers are omitted unless modern notes or matter are being cited.

> Plato, *Republic* 514a–520a.

Abbreviations of authors' names and works are extensively used in classical references. CMOS suggests following the abbreviation guidelines of the *Oxford Classical Dictionary*. Publication details should be provided in the first citation of a classical work (CMOS 14.246).

REFERENCE: Classical works are included in the bibliography only when the annotation or introduction of the specific edition is being cited, or the edition's translation itself is pertinent.

MLA   **CITATION:** When citing a classic work available in many editions, insert a semicolon after the page reference, then add the MLA abbreviations for volume (vol.), book (bk.), part (pt.), chapter (ch.), section (sec.), or paragraph (par.).

> Adam Smith argues that division of labor is at the root of the creation of societal wealth and well-being (9; bk. 1, ch. 1).

REFERENCE: No special rule. Make sure to specify the edition cited.

APA   **CITATION:** For the first citation, cite the version; subsequent citations of the text can leave out this information. Classical works usually have conventional divisions; these are more useful than page numbers.

> Ovid, *Metamorphoses*, 2:31–48.

> Plato, *Republic*, trans. B. Jowett, Book 1.

REFERENCE: Not usually included in the list of references.

50. The Bible or other religious works

CMOS   **CITATION/NOTE:** References to Jewish or Christian scriptures are usually limited to notes, and not included in the bibliography. For the first citation, identify the version; subsequent citations of the text can identify the version by abbreviation. Don't cite pages; instead, cite book, chapter, and verse.

Exod. 32:24 (New Revised Standard Version).

Numbers 14:4 (NRSV).

CMOS (10.45 to 10.48) includes lists of conventional abbreviations for versions and sections of the Bible.

REFERENCE: Scriptural references are usually not included in the bibliography.

MLA   **CITATION:** For the first citation, identify the version; subsequent citations of the text can leave out this information. Don't cite pages; instead, cite book, chapter, and verse.

"I threw it into the fire," Aaron says, "and out came this calf" (*New American Standard Bible*, Exod. 32:24).

REFERENCE: Identify the version.

New American Standard Bible. Collins-World, 1975.

APA   **CITATION:** For the first citation, identify the version and date of publication of that edition of that version (if known); subsequent citations of the text can leave out this information. Don't cite pages; instead, cite book, chapter, and verse.

"I threw it into the fire," Aaron says, "and out came this calf" (New American Standard Bible, 2018, Exodus 32.24).

REFERENCE: Not usually included in the list of references.

51. Poem

CMOS **CITATION/NOTE:** The first note specifies the edition and the format for line citations (including sections like books, cantos, or stanzas).
REFERENCE: No special rule.

MLA   **CITATION:** If the poem is short (no longer than a page), do not cite any number. If the poem is longer than a page, cite lines or other part numbers, but not page numbers (like this: "lines 87–93" or "book 3, line 57"). If the poem is longer than a page and is not published with explicit numbers marking lines or other parts, cite page numbers if available.

APA   **CITATION:** Note the general guidance earlier in this Appendix, in Quotations, on quoting and formatting poetry. Cite author, date

of publication, and stanza or section or line number(s), not page numbers.
REFERENCE: No special rule.

52. Drama

CMOS   **CITATION/NOTE:** The first note specifies the edition and the format for line citations.

> 1. *Antony and Cleopatra*, ed. Emrys Jones (London: Penguin, 1977), 5.2.279–80. References are to act, scene, and line(s).

> 2. *Antony and Cleopatra*, 2.5.42.

REFERENCE: Shakespeare, William. *Antony and Cleopatra*. Edited by Emrys Jones. New Penguin Shakespeare. London: Penguin, 1977.

MLA   **CITATION:** Provide page numbers or line numbers (line numbers are usually given after act and scene numbers) according to how the text is located in the edition.
REFERENCE: No special rule.

APA   **CITATION:** Note the general guidance earlier in this Appendix, in Quotations, on quoting and formatting drama.

Cite line act, scene, and line numbers, not page numbers: (1.2.128).
REFERENCE: No special rule.

53. Legal and government documents

CMOS   **CITATION/NOTE:** For legal and government documents, the 17th edition of CMOS suggests following the widely used *Bluebook* legal citation system, https://www.legalbluebook.com (accessible through most research libraries), even for works with a mainly nonlegal subject matter (CMOS 14.269).
REFERENCE: Legal-style citations following *Bluebook* style are not usually included in the bibliography.

MLA   Citing legal and government documents is complex, and the specifics may depend on whether you are a legal specialist or a student or scholar outside the legal profession. Generally, MLA style, in contrast with legal style, requires you to document the version of the work you consulted, not the "official" version of the law. For more information, see the *MLA Handbook*, section 2.1.3. Ask your teacher whether to follow a legal style like the *Bluebook*, and how specific documents and document types should be handled. Italicize the names of court cases. Capitalize laws, acts, and political documents in the same way as titles. In general, when in doubt treat legal documents like any source—identify author, title of source, title of container, version, number, publisher, publication or access date, and location, in the form of DOI or URL if appropriate. As always, your teacher is likely to provide guidance for particular complexities—if not, feel free to ask.

APA   There are many kinds of government reports, some issued by individuals, and some by agencies or other organizations. Consult the *APA Publication Manual* for full details. Here is the basic framework:

CITATION: (Government Author, Year, page or paragraph number, if applicable).

(U.S. Consumer Financial Protection Bureau and U.S. Department of Education, 2012, p. 4).

REFERENCE: Organization Name. (Year). *Title: Subtitle.* URL.

U.S. Consumer Financial Protection Bureau and U.S. Department of Education. (2012, July 20). *Private Student Loans: Report to the Senate Committee on Banking, Housing and Urban Affairs, the Senate Committee on Health, Education, Labor, and Pensions, the House of Representatives Committee on Financial Services, and the House of Representatives Committee on Education and the Workforce.* https://files.consumerfinance.gov/f/201207_cfpb _Reports_Private-Student-Loans.pdf

54. Congressional publication

CMOS   **CITATION/NOTE:** 1. *The Financial Collapse of Enron-Part 2: Hearing before the Subcomm. on Oversight and Investigations of the H. Comm. on Energy and Commerce*, 107th Cong. 41 (2002).

This note cites page 41 of the hearing transcript. Note that *Bluebook* style does not include the usual city and publisher information.

> **REFERENCE:** Bluebook citations are not usually included in the bibliography.

MLA **CITATION:** No special rule.
REFERENCE: Follow the standard MLA format template: government entity as author, title of source, publisher, date. You may include details about the congressional session or type of document.

> United States, Congress, Senate, Permanent Select Committee on Intelligence. *Russian Active Measures Campaigns and Interference in the 2016 U.S. Election.* Government Printing Office, 2019. 116th Congress, 1st session, Senate Report 116–20.

For a congressional document found online, provide the information for the document in one container. Then provide the name of the website, along with the DOI or URL.

APA **CITATION:** As for a general government publication.
REFERENCE: As for a general government publication.

55. Public law

CMOS **CITATION/NOTE:** When possible, cite the statutory code, not the public law. But if it is advised or more convenient to cite the public law, follow this format:

> Patient Protection and Affordable Care Act of 2010, Pub. L. No. 111-148, 124 Stat. 119.

REFERENCE: Not usually included in the bibliography.

MLA **CITATION:** Cite by a brief form of the title (matching how the item is alphabetized in the works-cited list).
REFERENCE: Follow the format for congressional publications. See the *MLA Handbook*, section 2.1.3 for more details.

APA **CITATION:** No special rule.
REFERENCE: Patient Protection and Affordable Care Act of 2010, Public Law No. 111-148. 124 Stat. 119 (2010). https://www.govinfo.gov/content/pkg/PLAW-111publ148/pdf/PLAW-111publ148.pdf

56. Indirect sources

Occasionally you may wish to cite an original source text cited in a work you've read even though you did not read the original source yourself (perhaps you did not have access to it). Such sources are called indirect sources. Generally, avoid citing indirect sources—if a text is important enough to cite, it's best to obtain it, read it, and cite it directly. But if that's not possible, you may occasionally cite indirect sources by following these guidelines.

CMOS   **CITATION/NOTE:** 1. W. E. B. Du Bois, *The Philadelphia Negro: A Social Study.* New Introduction by Herbert Atheker (Millwood, NY: Kraus-Thomson, 1973), 387, quoted in David Levering Lewis, *W. E. B. Du Bois: Biography of a Race* (New York: Henry Holt, 1993), 204.

              REFERENCE: List both the original and the secondary source (CMOS 14.260).

MLA   **CITATION:** Identify the direct source as well as the indirect source, using "qtd. in" (short for "quoted in").

              Du Bois acerbically summed up white attitudes toward black workingmen in *The Philadelphia Negro*: "Let them stagger downward" (qtd. in Lewis 204).

              REFERENCE: The indirect source is not included in the works-cited list; the direct source is.

              Lewis, David Levering. *W. E. B. Du Bois: Biography of a Race*, Henry Holt, 1993.

APA   **CITATION:** Identify the direct source as well as the indirect source, using "as cited in" or a similar phrase.

              Du Bois acerbically summed up white attitudes toward black workingmen in *The Philadelphia Negro*: "Let them stagger downward" (as cited in Lewis, 1993, p. 204).

              REFERENCE: The indirect source is not included in the reference list. The direct source is.

              Lewis, D. L. (1993). *W. E. B. Du Bois: Biography of a race.* Holt.

57. Missing information: no publisher or no place of publication

CMOS   **REFERENCE:** No place of publication: n.p. (or, following a period, N.p.) may be used before the publisher's name. Self-published books may not list a place of publication; in such cases, it is acceptable to simply omit the place of publication.

No publisher: n.p.

MLA   **REFERENCE:** Do not use placeholders for unknown information unless your teacher requires you to do so. For more details, see section 2.6.1 of the *MLA Handbook*.

APA   **REFERENCE:** No publisher: n.p. (APA 7th edition does not include place of publication.)

58. Missing information: no publication date

CMOS   **REFERENCE:** n.d.

London, n.d.

Or an approximate date may be included, with a question mark, in brackets: London, [1587?].

MLA   **REFERENCE:** Do not use placeholders for unknown information unless your teacher requires you to do so. For more details, see section 2.6.1 of the *MLA Handbook*.

APA   **REFERENCE:** n.d.

59. Missing information: no pages

CMOS   **CITATION/NOTE:** If no stable page numbers are available, cite by chapter or paragraph number if available, or by section heading. For short works such locators are not required.
REFERENCE: No special rule.

MLA   **CITATION:** No special rule. Use only the author's name in the citation, with no other numbers in place of page numbers.
REFERENCE: Do not use placeholders for unknown information unless your teacher requires you to do so. For more details, see section 2.6.1 of the *MLA Handbook*.

APA   **CITATION:** No special rule.

REFERENCE: Use a paragraph number if provided, or count paragraphs from the beginning of the document.

(Smith, 2010, para. 5).

1. Frequent reference to a single source

CMOS   **CITATION/NOTE:** If you quote or cite frequently from one text (this is likely to happen in a study of a literary text), give the full citation at the first mention, and then make subsequent citations parenthetically in the text. If citing drama or verse, it is helpful to include in the first note an explanation, such as "Text references are to act, scene, and line of this edition."

When several texts are frequently cited, it is advisable to include an abbreviation for each work in the parenthetical citation; a list of such abbreviations should be placed at the beginning or end of the work. This is rare in short papers, but common in long ones. (See CMOS 13.67.)

REFERENCE: No special rule.

MLA   **CITATION:** No special rule.
REFERENCE: No special rule.

APA   **CITATION:** No special rule.
REFERENCE: No special rule.

Works Cited

Works on Writing

Baker, Sheridon. *The Complete Stylist*. Thomas Crowell, 1966.

Bravmann, Scott. *Queer Fictions of the Past: History, Culture, and Difference*. Cambridge UP, 1997.

Corbett, Edward, and Robert Connors. *Classical Rhetoric for the Modern Student*. 4th ed., Oxford UP, 1998.

Fowler, Henry W. *A Dictionary of Modern English Usage*. 2nd ed., Oxford UP, 1983.

Ghent, Andra C., et al. "Complexity in Structured Finance." *The Review of Economic Studies*, vol. 86, no. 2, Mar. 2019, pp. 694–722, DOI:10.1093/restud/rdx071.

Harvey, Gordon. *Writing with Sources: A Guide for Students*. 3rd ed., Hackett, 2017.

Lanham, Richard. *Revising Prose*. 4th ed., Allyn & Bacon, 1999.

Orwell, George. "Politics and the English Language." *The Collected Essays, Journalism and Letters of George Orwell*, edited by Sonia Orwell and Ian Angus, vol. 4, Harcourt Brace, 1968, pp. 127–41.

———. "Why I Write." *The Orwell Reader*. Harcourt Brace, 1956, pp. 390–96.

Weston, Anthony. *A Rulebook for Arguments*. 5th ed., Hackett, 2017.

Williams, Joseph M. *Style: Ten Lessons in Clarity and Grace*. 4th ed., HarperCollins, 1994.

Other Works

Booth, William. "Collective Conscience." *Washington Post*, 22 Aug. 1999, pp. B1, B5.

CNN Newsroom. CNN transcript #011500CN.V05, 15 Jan. 2002. Retrieved 15 Apr. 2003 from LexisNexis database.

Hackett, Darren. "Lawyers Toil for Two Decades Trying to Break the Maryland Code." *Washington Post*, 26 Aug. 1989, pp. B1, B5.

Mitric, Joan. "The Environment as Prisoner of War." *Washington Post*, 9 July 2000, pp. B1, B4.

Pentagon Briefing. CNN transcript #99040810FN–105, 8 Apr. 1999. Retrieved 15 Apr. 2003 from LexisNexis database.

"The President's Testimony: Part Four of Eight." *New York Times*, 22 Sept. 1998, p. B3.

Rosenthal, Elisabeth. "In China's Legal Evolution, the Lawyers Are Handcuffed." *New York Times*, 6 Jan. 2000, pp. A1, A10.

"Terms of Discourse." *Journal of Animal Ethics*, vol. 1, no. 1, Spring 2011, pp. vii–ix.

Tidwell, Mike. "Found at Sea: Seeking an Obscure Haven in a Tourist-Soaked Region, a Traveler Gets Himself Seriously Marooned on a Desert Island." *Washington Post*, 28 Feb. 1999, pp. E1, E6–8.